essential

80s

pop quiz

Kirstin all the very best :: Thanks for coming! Thea x

by

thea newcomb

First published in Great Britain in 1998 by

TNP
355 Byres Road, Suite 114
Glasgow G12 8QZ

info: tnp-books@mailcity.com

A catalogue record for this book is available from the British Library.

ISBN 0 9534124 0 7

Original cover design by Mark Di Meo.

Printed and bound in Great Britain by
The Cromwell Press, Wiltshire.

For Ralph Newcomb,
the best father in the world,
for all of his love and endless support.
Thanks dad!

Also in loving memory of my mother
Glenda Rae who always said I would write...

Fair Dues

My biggest debt of gratitude goes to Derick Turner for all of his unwavering faith in me - not to mention his unconditional love and support. In the honourable words of the Style Council - "You're The Best Thing". : o)

Thanks to my entire family and Derick's family too!

Additionally, it's my turn to acknowledge a few of my true friends - and some colleagues who have helped me out at one point or another in my career:

Donna Aal, Frank Andrick, Victoria Barnett, Yvonne Barron@Zipo (we did it!), Ken Braasch, Sharon Curtis, Bonnie Datt, Marco Di Meo, John Dingwall, Carol DuPuis, Brian Ford, John Gallagher, Heather & Gerry George, Kimberly (the best friend I've never met)Geschke, Shona Graham, Jenny Hunter, Kim (Spangle) Iden, Karen Jones, Sabine Jones, Fiona Kemp, Jim Knell, Brian Kurtz, Carol Laula, Lori Lehtola, Audrey Lillie, Marie McNeilly, Hannah Markham, Geoff Martyn, Elizabth Medel, Fraser Middleton, Mairi Munn, David Wesley Page, Dawn & Kevin Pinnt, Sandra Robertson, Tim Seward, Derek Smith, Sally Stratton, Cristin Thompson, Amanda Tobier, Tara Waddell, and Wee Fat Bob!

Sincere apologies to those I have omitted, of which I am sure there are many. It was for no other reason than lack of space (and remaining active brain cells at this point!).

Last, but by no means least, Neil Moyes for his generousity and for helping me make this happen. Many thanks for your support!.

The Categories

VINYL SOLUTIONS -- Questions about albums.

ALL IN A NAME -- Origins of band or artist names.

SINGLE-MINDED -- Singles questions, of course.

POTLUCK -- Is self-explanitory (I hope)..

CELLULOID & THE BOX -- Film and TV questions.

BANDSTAND -- Questions pertaining to bands, soloists, off- shoots, and collaborations.

FLASHBACK FAVOURITES -- (My favourite category) - contains "hits", "misses" and college radio "classics".

WONDERS OF THE WORLD -- is a term I use very loosely. A band could have had one hit in the US and ten in the UK (or vice versa) and they may still be in this category. The question should be worded to indicate that.

UNDER-COVER -- The very last quiz is simply cover versions of other peoples' songs.

 # 1 -- Stands for Number One and are broken in to Albums, Singles, US and UK.

Note: It is important to note that album and movie titles are in italics, and quotes are around "Singles" and "TV Shows". Also # = "Number.".

Introduction

Warning! This book is not for the musically-challenged but rather for those who love to be challenged, musically. If you don't know the difference between Yaz (aka Yazoo) and Yazz, then this book *may not* be for you. It has an "Alternative" slant and a British bias too. However, a large portion of the questions are North American, with some Australian and European bands thrown in for good measure.

If you get half of the answers in the book, you are doing pretty well. If you get more than half, you really know your stuff. If you get most or all of them, either you're a genius or you cheated! I wrote the book and I can't even get all of the answers! Though, what would be the point in making it an easy quiz?

Having been a long time fan of music, especially '80s music, I began to write this book a few years back. It was only recently that I decided it was the "right" time to give up my job in order to finish it. Let's face it, the '80s are *hot* right now. Judging by some recent movie releases and the sheer abundance of '80s music compilations, there must be a lot of people out there, like me, who have a passion for the '80s - with all its crazy music and fashion sense...

If I have done my job well, this book should bring back some of those memories that have long since been forgotten, and it should continually give your long-term memory a work-out. This book will hopefully be fun, but at the same time, you just may learn something...

All of the questions came from my own music collection (well, what was left after being robbed earlier this year), with the assistance of many music reference books (see sources p.191), the Internet and by watching an endless stream of videos (you can learn a lot from watching "Pop-Up Video"!). It is my intention that this book be used as an ice-breaker at parties or maybe in pubs. It's handy for bus, tube, train, car and plane journeys - I know, I've tried it! Broadcasters may want to use it to fill some air time - that's fine provided you plug the book! :) You can quiz yourself or your friends - it's *"fun for the whole family"*. Well,...maybe not the "whole" family.

Hopefully, you will enjoy it as much as I did writing it. Undoubtedly, you will see that there are some missing "classics" here, but that is both inevitable and unavoidable, I'm afraid. Perhaps they'll be in the next one...?

Disclaimer: Though every effort was made to fact-check this book thoroughly, mistakes do happen. If you find any blatantly wrong questions/answers (eg. not just typos), please feel free to show-off, by emailing them to:

essential-80s@mailcity.com.

Have Fun!

Vinyl Solutions

1. Their only US hit was the 1982 album *Non-Stop Erotic Cabaret.*

2. Which Scottish band released the UK Top 5 *Southside* in 1989?

3. Who released the *Conscious Party* in 1988?

4. *Picture Book* was whose debut hit album?

5. *The Youth Of Today* was their 1983 album.

6. Which quartet released *Stop Making Sense* in 1984?

7. Who followed up their self-titled debut with *Talk Talk Talk?*

8. *Once Upon A Time* was a US Top 10 for them.

9. Their 1984 album was simply called *Pop.*

10. Who released *The Colour Of Spring* in the Spring of '86?

Flashback Favourites

1. "Birds Fly (Whisper To A Scream)" was whose 1984 single?

2. Which former member of Magazine recorded the ethereal "Rainy Season"?

3. Name the band that sang "Hand On My Heart" in 1984.

4. Who sang "Swear" in 1983?

5. They sang "AEIOU Sometimes Y" in 1984.

6. "Chamber Of Hellos" and "I'll Do You" were college radio classics by which Californian band?

7. In 1988, which Dublin band sang "Call Me Blue"?

8. Whose 1987 sad tale was entitled "Hope Road"?

9. "Baby's In The Mountains" was a single from who in 1983?

10. In 1984 Robert Görl of DAF released "Darling Don't Leave Me" - which cropped-haired songstress helped on vocals?

Quiz #3

Single-Minded

1. Who sang "Like An Animal" in 1983?

2. They followed their US hit "Voices Carry" with another "What About Love" in 1986.

3. Whose first US hit was "Keep On Movin"?

4. What was the name of Public Image Limited's anti-love hit in 1983?

5. Their "I Wanna Be A Flintstone" had international appeal in 1988.

6. The biggest UK hit for them was "The Word Girl" in 1985.

7. Whose "Relax" was in the UK chart for four months?

8. Twice they had a UK Top 20 hit with "Love Will Tear Us Apart".

9. Who sang "I Don't Want To Be A Hero" and "Shattered Dreams"?

10. "My Ever Changing Moods" was their only US hit.

Potluck

1. Who took *The Road To Hell* to the top of the UK charts in 1989?

2. In 1987 these former members of Japan released a single called "Buoy".

3. Simply Red topped the US charts twice in the '80s - name either track.

4. *La Bamba* was the name of whose US chart-topping album and single?

5. Whose name is derived from the phrase "kiss my ass" in Gaelic?

6. At one time, this New Romantic band featured Stephen "Tin Tin" Duffy.

7. Which Austrian band featured their name in the title of their 1989 UK Top 5 hit?

8. John Lennon said they were his favourite band in 1980.

9. Both the Eurythmics and Madonna had a single with the same title, in '83 and '87 respectively - what is it?

10. Who worked with the Gang Of Four and Alison Moyet before starting Fairground Attraction?

Quiz #5

Vinyl Solutions

1. *The Lion And The Cobra* was the debut from who?

2. "Favourite Shirts" and "Love Plus One" were hit singles from which Haircut 100 album?

3. Name the Californian band who released *Mother's Milk* in 1989.

4. Who had a UK hit in 1983 with *Deep Sea Skiving*?

5. *Outlandos D'Amour* and *Reggatta De Blanc* were hit albums from which British trio?

6. Whose debut album was *The Crossing*?

7. *Kissing To Be Clever* and *Waking Up With The House On Fire* were hit albums from who?

8. Who was *Hunting High & Low* in 1985?

9. Their 1985 album was ...*All The Rage*.

10. Whose early releases included *Construction Time Again* and *Speak And Spell*?

Bandstand

1. Debbie Harry used to front which American band?

2. Alison Moyet and Vince Clarke were known as what?

3. Name the Los Angeles band that featured Peter Case.

4. What is the name of the band Peter Murphy fronted in the '80s?

5. Maria McKee was the lead woman in this '80s band.

6. Feargal Sharkey was in which Irish band?

7. Porno For Pyro's Perry Farrell was the founding member of which '80s band?

8. Tom Bailey, Alannah Currie and Joe Leeway were known as what?

9. David Baerwald and David Ricketts made up which Los Angeles Rock duo?

10. What Scottish band was Karl Wallinger a member of before World Party?

Quiz #7

Single-Minded

1. Who sang "Since Yesterday" in 1984?

2. "Tomorrow People" was their first UK hit.

3. "Rock Lobster" and "Private Idaho" are classic tracks by who?

4. Which New Romantic band sang "We Came To Dance" and "Dancing With Tears In My Eyes"?

5. "Candybar Express" was the first UK hit for which Glasgow Pop band?

6. They were "Calling All The Heroes" in 1986.

7. Who was "Close (To The Edit)" in 1984?

8. "Mexican Radio" was their 1983 UK hit.

9. They had UK # 2 hits with both "Cool For Cats" and "Up The Junction".

10. Who was "Making Plans For Nigel" in 1979?

Celluloid & The Box

1. Who did the title track to the film *Never Ending Story*?

2. In 1989 their US Top 10 "Room To Move" was featured in *My Stepmother's An Alien*.

3. Whose hit "Romancing The Stone" wasn't actually in the film?

4. She appeared in *Valley Girl* performing her 1982 single "Johnny Are You Queer?".

5. Whose "Buffalo Stance" was featured in the film *Slaves Of New York*?

6. In 1985 they topped the US charts with the title song to *A View To A Kill.*

7. The film *Howard The Duck* featured whose music?

8. Which band did the soundtrack to the film *To Live And Die In LA*?

9. *Nuns On The Run* is a film that featured whose UK Top 10 hit "The Race"?

10. They did the title track to the film *The Living Daylights* in 1987.

Quiz #9

Vinyl Solutions

1. Whose 1986 compilation was called *Street Life 20 Great Hits*?

2. Her debut *Ancient Heart* was a UK # 3.

3. Whose solo UK hit was the 1989 album *Read My Lips*?

4. The 1987 album *Babble* was a UK Top 30 hit for who?

5. *Brilliant Trees* was whose 1984 debut solo album?

6. Which Anglo-American band released *Let It Bee* in 1988?

7. Who had UK chart success with their 1988 *What Up Dog* album?

8. The 1985 album *World Service* was nearly a Top 10 hit in the UK for who?

9. Whose 1981 US hit album was *The Completion Backward Principle*?

10. *Sunshine On Leith* was whose UK Top 10 album?

All In A Name

1. What is Elvis Costello's real name?

2. Which German Synth band took their name from a 1965 French sci-fi film?

3. Frank Tovey's pseudonymn is what?

4. Which Glasgow band's name is said to be Greek for "Into The Womb"?

5. How is Buzzcock Howard Trafford best known?

6. This Irish band's name means "family" in Gaelic.

7. Which English band took their name from a Russian ballet company?

8. Who is Hugh Cregg III?

9. This Manchester band took their name from a rough area in Glasgow.

10. How is William Wolfe Broad best known?

Bandstand

1. Marc Almond and David Ball were known as what?

2. Which Canadian band features siblings Margo, Michael and Peter Timmons?

3. This trio featured two guys named Paul and their debut was *A Walk Across The Rooftops*.

4. Difford & Tillbrook were members of which English Pop band?

5. This Brisbane band featured the talents of Grant McLennan and Robert Forster.

6. Which duo featured Neil Arthur and Steven Luscombe?

7. Thurston Moore and Kim Gordon were from which New York band?

8. Dave Wakeling and Rankin' Roger formed the core of General Public - what was their previous band?

9. This Welsh band featured twins Jay and Michael Aston.

10. Peter Zaremba was lead man in which New York band?

Single-Minded

1. He sang the UK # 1 “Nineteen” in ‘85.

2. In 1988 “Rok Da House” was a UK # 5 hit for who?

3. Their first UK Top 10 was “Happy Hour” in 1986.

4. In 1988 it was second time lucky with “Voyage Voyage” for this French vocalist.

5. “Don’t Call Me Baby” was whose UK Top 20 single?

6. She was a “Slave To The Rhythm” in 1985.

7. Who followed up their chart-topping UK hit with “Come Back And Stay” in 1983?

8. They sang “On My Radio” in 1979.

9. Their second UK hit was “No Sleep Till Brooklyn” in 1987.

10. Who released the 1987 UK hit “Stutter Rap (No Sleep ‘Til Bedtime)”?

Vinyl Solutions

1. Whose only UK hit album was *Shangri-La* in 1985?

2. In 1982 they released the UK Top 10 *Fabrique*.

3. *Punch The Clock* was the 1983 hit album from who?

4. In 1984 who had the UK hit album *Sisters*?

5. *Dig The New Breed* was the follow-up to whose UK # 1 *The Gift*?

6. *Blue Sunshine* was their UK Top 20 hit in 1983.

7. Their only album was *Where The Action Is*.

8. Which British duo had a UK hit with *Everything* in 1988?

9. *Oil On Canvas* was the only UK Top 10 album by who?

10. Whose 1984 debut was the hit album *She's So Unusual*?

Quiz #14

Wonders Of The World

1. Whose only UK hit was "Big In Japan"?

2. "Tantalise (Wo Wo Ee Yeh Yeh)" was the UK Top 20 hit for who in 1983?

3. Two one-hit wonders had hits with "Funky Town" (aka "Funkytown") - name either.

4. Who had a hit with "Tarzan Boy" in 1985?

5. In 1980 who sang "Echo Beach"?

6. Whose only UK hit was "Obsession" in 1985?

7. This British duo had moderate success with "Shooting From My Heart".

8. Which Australian band's UK hit was "That's When I Think Of You"?

9. "Pump Up The Volume" was a UK # 1 and their only hit.

10. Whose cover of "Can't Help Falling In Love" was a 1986 UK hit?

Quiz #15

UK # 1 Albums

1. *Let's Dance* was one of the UK chart-toppers by who?

2. Name the chart-topping Duran Duran album that featured the singles "The Reflex" and "Union Of The Snake".

3. *Welcome To The Pleasuredome* was a hit album for who in 1984?

4. Their *Technique* topped the charts in 1989.

5. What was the name of Peter Gabriel's # 1 album from 1986?

6. Name the Smiths' chart-topping album from 1985.

7. *Boys & Girls* was the 1985 chart-topper for who?

8. Who released the hit album *Dare* in 1981?

9. Whose *Legend* was a chart-topper in 1984?

10. *Nothing Like The Sun* was the only UK # 1 in the '80s for who?

Flashback Favourites

1. Who sang such classics as “Homosapien” and “Telephone Operator”?

2. Who had a “Lost Weekend” in 1985?

3. In 1988 who had a hit with “Tears Run Rings”?

4. “Be With You” was a single from who in 1987?

5. Who sang the 1980 UK hit “Banana Republic”?

6. “The Great Commandment” was a single by who?

7. This band asked “What For?” in 1988.

8. “Twist” and “Go” were tracks by which Bauhaus spin-off?

9. Whose 1988 single “Victoria” was a UK hit?

10. They sang “Certain Things Are Likely” in 1987.

Vinyl Solutions

1. Whose debut was the UK Top 5 *White Feathers*?

2. They followed up *Love* with *Electric*.

3. Who released their first album *A Letter From St. Paul* in 1987?

4. Whose debut album was entitled *Liquidizer*?

5. *Blue* was the 1986 debut for who?

6. Which American Rock band followed up their self-titled debut with the 1986 album *Shelter*?

7. In 1983 who released a Synth-Pop album *With Sympathy*?

8. *What's That Noise* was the only hit album for who?

9. Which Canadian outfit released *The Rhythm Of Youth* in 1983?

10. *Silvertone* was whose 1985 debut?

Quiz #18

Celluloid & The Box

1. The film *Less Than Zero* featured their cover of "Hazy Shade Of Winter".

2. "Because Of You" was the theme from the UK TV show "Brushstrokes"- who sang it?

3. Whose "Love Kills" was taken from the *Sid & Nancy* soundtrack?

4. Their single "Iko Iko" was a US hit from *Rain Man.*

5. "Eye Of The Tiger" was whose massive hit from Stallone's *Rocky III*?

6. Who appeared in Olivia Newton-John's *Xanadu* and later had a US Top 10 with "She's A Beauty"?

7. They sang "Dancing In Heaven (Orbital Be Bop)" from the Sarah Jessica Parker film *Girls Just Wanna Have Fun*.

8. Whose 1988 UK hit single "I'm Gonna Be (500 Miles)" became a massive US hit from the 1993 film *Benny And Joon*?

9. Who did the soundtrack to the film adaptation of Orwell's *1984*?

10. Their first UK hit was the "Theme From Harry's Game" in 1982.

Quiz #19

Single-Minded

1. Who sang "Rock This Town" in 1982?

2. They had a UK hit in 1987 with "Ideal World".

3. "Cry Boy Cry" was their UK Top 20 in 1982.

4. Who first had success with "Pop Musik" in 1979?

5. Their debut was the UK Top 10 "Crash".

6. The first hit "We Close Our Eyes" was their biggest.

7. In 1987 "The Motive (Living Without You)" was their UK hit.

8. Who followed up "Good Tradition" with "Twist In My Sobriety"?

9. He released consecutive UK Top 40 hits "Imagination" and "Some People" in 1986.

10. Who had a hit with "Yeh Yeh" in 1985?

Quiz #20

Bandstand

1. Ian Brown and John Squire were members of which successful Manchester band in the '80s?

2. Garbage's Shirley Manson used to sing in this Edinburgh-based band.

3. Aimee Mann used to be in which Boston band?

4. Producer Mitch Easter founded which North Carolina band in 1981?

5. UK TV presenter Richard Jobson and Stuart Adamson were members of which Scottish New Wave band?

6. Paul Westerberg used to front this Minneapolis band.

7. Vocalist Mike Scott used to front which Celtic Rock band?

8. Juliana Hatfield used to be in which late-'80s band?

9. Mark Eitzel founded which influential San Francisco band?

10. Stan Ridgeway had a UK Top 5 with "Camouflage" - what was his '80s band called?

Quiz #21

Vinyl Solutions

1. Whose only UK hit album was *North Of A Miracle*?

2. *Solitude Standing* was this New Yorker's 1987 release.

3. Which Scottish band debuted with *Psychocandy* in 1985?

4. They released *Battle Hymns For Children Singing* in 1983.

5. Who released *Dream Of The Blue Turtles* in 1985?

6. Both *The Raven* and *Feline* were UK # 4 hits for who?

7. *If You Want To Defeat Your Enemy Sing His Song* was the UK Top 30 album from them.

8. This Boston band released *Hunkpapa* in 1989.

9. *Still* and *Closer* were hit albums from which Manchester band?

10. In 1989 who were *Taking On The World* with their debut?

Quiz #22

Flashback Favourites

1. Like the Art of Noise and Tom Jones, this noisy Leeds band covered Prince's "Kiss".

2. Which Minneapolis band sang "Love Is The Law" in 1983?

3. This New York duo sang "Don't Let's Start".

4. This Scottish band sang "I Love The Things You Do To Me" in 1987.

5. Whose "Collapsing New People" was a UK Indie chart Top 5 hit?

6. "Punk Rock Girl" was a quirky number from which Philadelphia band?

7. Two of this band's classics were "Kiss Off" and "Blister In The Sun".

8. Who had "Love And Pride" in '85?

9. "Take The Skinheads Bowling" was a 1986 single by who?

10. This Australian outfit sang "If You Leave Me, Can I Come Too?" in 1982.

UK # 1 Singles

1. Who sang “Geno” in 1980?

2. Which Scot topped the UK charts with “Japanese Boy”?

3. “Never Gonna Give You Up” was his only UK chart-topper.

4. Whose Double A-side featured “Computer Love” b/w “The Model” and topped the UK chart in 1981?

5. Their single was “Perfect” in 1988.

6. Who sang “Don’t Turn Around” in 1988?

7. “Going Underground” was the first of four # 1 hits for the Jam - name one of the other three.

8. In 1984 who had a # 1 with “99 Red Balloons”?

9. Who topped the UK charts with “Brass In Pocket”?

10. “True” was a hit for who?

Quiz #24

Single-Minded

1. "Love Train" and "Americanos" were both UK # 4 hits for who?

2. Who debuted with "Shattered Dreams"?

3. "Only The Lonely" was a US Top 10 hit for this Los Angeles band.

4. His debut was a hit single called "New Song".

5. Whose biggest UK hit in the '80s was "Drop The Pilot"?

6. Which British trio scored a debut hit with "Breakout"?

7. Their first hit was their biggest, "Party Fears Two" in '82.

8. "Can Can" and "Special Brew" were both UK # 3 hits for who?

9. In 1985 who was "Running Up That Hill"?

10. Which English band had a hit with "Der Kommisar" in 1983?

Quiz #25

Vinyl Solutions

1. *Scared To Dance* and *The Absolute Game* were both UK Top 20 hits for who?

2. Whose debut album was *Private Revolution*?

3. The 1988 album *The Frenz Experiment* was whose UK Top 20?

4. They released such UK hit albums as *Happy Familie*s and *Mange Tout*.

5. Who were *Seduced & Abandoned* in 1987?

6. *Ricochet Days* and *After The Snow* were albums from which English outfit?

7. This former Policeman called his 1987 album *X,Y,Z*.

8. Which Scottish band had *Fisherman's Blues* in 1988?

9. *People* reached # 2 in the UK for who?

10. Their 1988 album was *All That Jazz*.

Potluck

1. Who co-wrote "Love Like A Rocket" with Bob Geldof?

2. He got his start selling Levi jeans and recorded the UK Top 5 hit "Each Time You Break My Heart".

3. Who sang the Top 10 hit "Walk The Dinosaur"?

4. Name the Sinead O'Connor single that is featured in the film *Married To The Mob.*

5. There are two different singles called "Dear God", Midge Ure's one - name the other.

6. Which beverage was Mike craving in Suicidal Tendencies' "Institutionalized"?

7. "Last Christmas" is the seasonal hit from who?

8. What was the name of the hit single by the Artists United Against Apartheid?

9. This 1983 Eurovision contestant went on to release the 1988 UK hit "Im Nin'Alu".

10. Who had an album and single called *Forever Young*?

Quiz #27

Wonders Of The World

1. "The Captain Of Her Heart" was which Swiss band's hit?

2. "Doot Doot" was a moderate UK hit for who in 1983?

3. Who had an '80s hit with the 1920's song "Puttin' On The Ritz"?

4. "I Know There's Something Going On" was a hit in for who in 1982?

5. They nearly topped the US charts with "Keep Your Hands To Yourself".

6. Who had a hit "One Night In Bangkok"?

7. Their only US hit was "Turning Japanese" in 1980.

8. Who had a UK hit with "Magic Smile" in 1987?

9. "10-9-8" was the only US hit for this Boston band.

10. "I Can't Wait" was the only UK Top 40 hit for who?

Quiz #28

Single-Minded

1. They first had success with "There She Goes" in 1989.

2. Who sang "What I Am"?

3. "What's On Your Mind (Pure Energy)" was the US Top 5 hit for who?

4. Whose US hits in the '80s were "Don't Dream It's Over" and "Something So Strong"?

5. They had two US hits "Life In A Northern Town" and "The Love Parade".

6. "Under The Milkyway" was whose only US hit?

7. Their US hit in the '80s was "Tenderness".

8. Who sang "I Love You" in 1983?

9. "I Want To Be Free" and "Thunder In The Mountains" were UK Top 10 hits for who?

10. In 1985 who sang "Love Is Just The Great Pretender"?

Vinyl Solutions

1. *Strip Mine* was the follow-up to their 1986 album *Stutter.*

2. Whose US debut hit was *Picture This*?

3. Who was *Talking With The Taxman About Poetry* in 1986?

4. *Reckoning* and *Fables Of The Reconstruction* were early releases from which band?

5. *Human Racing* was the first of two albums released by Nik Kershaw in 1984 - what was the second?

6. *Rip It Up* was the second 1982 UK Top 40 album for who?

7. *Happy Head* and *The World Without End* are two albums from who?

8. This Glasgow trio released *Strange Kind Of Love* in 1988.

9. Whose *Kite* was a UK Top 40 hit?

10. They followed up *Power, Corruption & Lies* with *Low-Life.*

Quiz #30

All In A Name

1. This band's name means "fast fashion" in French.

2. What is Boy George's real name?

3. How are Paul Hewson and Dave Evans better known?

4. David Robert Jones is best known as who?

5. Which Liverpool band took their name from a Wild West "Wanted" poster?

6. Helen Folasade Adu goes by what name?

7. This Minnesota band took their name from a Swedish board game and translates as "do you remember?".

8. Who is Stuart Goddard better known as?

9. Who is Georgios Kyriacos Panayiotou?

10. This Liverpool Synth band's name was inspired by a title of a famous Richard Bach book.

Quiz #31

Bandstand

1. Sisters Rose and Rachel Carlotti made up half of which Reading band?

2. Name the Scottish band that featured Robert Hodgens and brothers Ken and Dave McCluskey.

3. Johnny Thunders, David Johansen, Arthur Harold Kane and Sylvain Sylvain are best known as who?

4. Malcolm McLaren created this band which featured his protégée Annabella Lu Win on vocals.

5. Steve Severin and Robert Smith united for this 1983 project.

6. Andy McCluskey and Paul Humphreys were the core members of which British band?

7. American sisters Tracey Bryn and Melissa Belland teamed up with Woody and Bedders from Madness to form which band?

8. Siblings Jim and William Reid are the core members of this Scottish band.

9. In which band would you find Kate Pierson and Fred Schneider?

10. What band featured Dave Stewart and Annie Lennox prior to the Eurythmics?

Quiz #32

Single-Minded

1. Whose first US hit was "Cruel Summer"?

2. "Anchorage" was her song from 1988.

3. Whose first hit "Fade To Grey" was their biggest?

4. In 1988 this trio nearly had a US Top 10 with "The Promise".

5. "Hey Matthew" was a UK Top 10 for who in 1987?

6. Their "We Care A Lot" single was a UK hit in 1988.

7. Who had a hit with "Won't Talk About It" in 1989?

8. Who was "Waiting For A Train" in 1983?

9. Who sang "Can't Be Sure" in 1989?

10. "Blue Kiss" was a single by who in 1985?

Vinyl Solutions

1. In 1985 *Love Not Money* was a UK Top 10 for who?

2. Who followed up their self-titled debut with *Nothing's Shocking*?

3. *Aliens Ate My Buick* was the follow-up to whose UK Top 20 *The Flat Earth*?

4. In 1989 she followed up her self-titled debut with *Porcelain*.

5. Who followed up *Hang Ten* with *This Is Our Art* in 1988?

6. Whose 1986 debut album *Inside* featured some members of the Banshees, Heartbreakers, Bangles and Aimee Mann too?

7. They followed up their self-titled debut with *Waiting* in 1983.

8. At Christmas in 1985, who charted with *So The Red Rose*?

9. Which English Pop band followed up *Labour Of Love* with *Geffrey Morgan*?

10. Which Minnesota band released their *Let It Be* album in 1984?

UK # 1 Singles

1. Their only # 1 hit in the '80s was a cover of the Beatle's "With A Little Help From My Friends".

2. In 1979 "I Don't Like Mondays" was a chart-topping hit for them.

3. "Happy Talk" jumped to the top of the charts in 1982 for who?

4. They scored big with their cover of the Yaz(oo) hit "Only You".

5. Who were "Too Shy" in 1983?

6. "If I Was" was whose # 1?

7. Their only chart-topper was a cover of Lennon's "Jealous Guy".

8. Whose debut "Ride On Time" was a UK # 1?

9. "The Only Way Is Up" was their # 1 in the Summer of '88.

10. Dead Or Alive topped the UK charts only once - name it.

Celluloid & The Box

1. He recorded the title track to the John Hughes film *She's Having A Baby*.

2. Who sang the title track to the Molly Ringwald film *Pretty In Pink*?

3. From *Pretty In Pink*, whose hit "Left Of Center" featured Joe Jackson on piano?

4. "If You Leave" was whose hit from *Pretty In Pink*?

5. Simple Mind's "Don't You (Forget About Me)" was a hit from which Brat Pack film?

6. *Uncle Buck* featured whose 1988 version of "Wild Thing"?

7. Whose single "I Go Crazy" was in the film *Some Kind Of Wonderful*?

8. *Say Anything* prominently featured whose track "In Your Eyes"?

9 Whose singles "Whistle Down The Wind" and "When It Started To Begin" are played at the dance in *16 Candles*?

10. Name the Californian band who did the theme tune to the film *Weird Science*.

Potluck

1. Which guitar legend can be found on the Art of Noise's "Peter Gunn"?

2. *Birth, School, Work, Death* is both an album and single from which Gothic band?

3. Feargal Sharkey had huge success with "A Good Heart" - who wrote it?

4. *Boys Don't Cry* is the name of both an album and single from which British band?

5. Whose *Fur* album spawned the hit single "Rush Hour"?

6. *Happy Birthday* was both an album and single by who?

7. Whose vocals are featured on Electronic's "Getting Away With It"?

8. Who collaborated with Clannad on the hit "In A Lifetime"?

9. Which popular icon directed Curiousity Killed The Cat's "Misfit" video?

10. Who sang the UK hit "Cross That Bridge" in 1987?

Vinyl Solutions

1. Name the Scottish band whose debut was *High Land Hard Rain*.

2. In 1988 who had the UK Top 10 album *Close*?

3. Whose 1981 *Anthem* was a near UK chart-topper?

4. *Strength* and *Declaration* were early albums by who?

5. Who was *In Heat* in 1983?

6. Which Glasgow band released *Raintown* in 1988?

7. *This Is The Day, This Is The Hour, This Is This* was the 1989 release from which English band?

8. *Whose Side Are You On?* was the debut album from who?

9. *Candleland* was whose UK Top 20 album and featured a single of the same name.

10. In 1981 *Quit Dreaming And Get On The Beam* was a UK Top 10 for who?

Single-Minded

1. Which Australian outfit scored a UK Top 20 with "Hey Little Girl" in 1983?

2. "Love Resurrection" and "All Cried Out" were hits for who?

3. Who had a UK Top 5 hit with "Eloise" in 1986?

4. "Show Me" and "Don't Get Me Wrong" were hit singles by who?

5. "My Perfect Cousin" and "Jimmy Jimmy" were two of their UK hits.

6. Whose biggest single was "The Honeythief" in 1986?

7. "WFL" (aka "Wrote For Luck") was their UK chart debut in 1989.

8. Who sang "All Around The World" in 1989?

9. In 1983 they "Just Got Lucky" with a UK Top 10.

10. Who had a hit with "Buffalo Gals" in 1982?

Quiz #39

Wonders Of The World

1. Who was at the "Breaking Point" in 1984?

2. "Dance Hall Days" was their only UK hit.

3. Who had a hit with "Rumors" in 1986?

4. Their UK hit was "Brilliant Mind".

5. Who sang the US hit "I Wanna Be A Cowboy" in 1986?

6. "Let's Go All The Way" was the only hit for who?

7. This Welsh band had a US Top 10 with "Cry" in 1989.

8. Whose only US hit was "Perfect Way"?

9. "Major Tom (Coming Home)" was the name of his only US hit.

10. Who sang the quirky single "Homecoming Queen's Got A Gun"?

Flashback Favourites

1. In 1982 which band released "Animal Song"?

2. They sang a number about Brian Jones called "Godstar".

3. "I Want You" was a 1985 club hit from which Sheffield band?

4. Who released the single "Harley Davidson (Son Of A Bitch)" in 1986?

5. Who sang "My Boyfriend" in 1983?

6. Whose club hit was entitled "The Dominatrix Sleeps To-night"?

7. "Einstein A Go-Go" was their 1981 UK Top 5 hit.

8. Their first UK hit was "Down To Earth".

9. Which Sydney quartet released "Slave Girl" in 1985?

10. They sang the 1984 single "Burning Flame".

Quiz #41

Vinyl Solutions

1. *Please* was the UK debut hit album by who?

2. *Architecture & Morality* and *Dazzle Ships* were UK Top 5 hits for who?

3. Whose debut *Diamond Life* nearly topped the UK charts?

4. Who followed up *Rebel Yell* with *Whiplash Smile*?

5. *Doolittle* was this Boston band's 1989 album.

6. Who debuted with *Steps In Time*?

7. They followed up *First (The Sound Of Music)* with *The Big Area* in 1989.

8. Whose debut *Spring Session M* was an anagram of their name?

9. In 1984 they had their highest charting album *It'll End In Tears*?

10. *Tinderbox* was the name of their 1986 album.

Quiz #42

UK # 1 Albums

1. Who blasted to the top of the UK charts with *Blast*?

2. *Turn Back The Clock* was a UK # 1 from who?

3. Who took *Into The Gap* to the top of the charts?

4. *Alf* was the UK chart-topper for who in 1984?

5. Who had chart-topping *Faith* in 1987?

6. *Replicas*, *The Pleasure Principle* and *Telekon* were all UK # 1 albums by who?

7. *Human's Lib* was whose album which entered the UK chart in the top spot?

8. *Viva Hate* was whose solo debut and UK # 1 album?

9. *Ghost In The Machine* and *Zenyatta Mondatta* were two of five consecutive UK # 1 albums by who?

10. *Flesh & Blood* and *Avalon* were their consecutive UK chart-toppers.

Quiz #43

Single-Minded

1. Whose single was "Too Good To Be Forgotten" in 1986?

2. In 1980 "Train In Vain" was the first of two US hits for who?

3. Their single "(Feels Like) Heaven" was a UK Top 10 in 1984.

4. "Don't Forget Me (When I'm Gone)" was a hit for who in 1986?

5. "I.O.U." was nearly a UK # 1 for who in 1983?

6. "Johnny Come Home" was their first UK hit single.

7. "The Message" and "White Lines (Don't Do It)" were early '80s hits by who?

8. Who sang "Like The Weather" in 1987?

9. "Is She Really Going Out With Him?" was whose 1979 hit?

10. He had the instrumental hit "Rockit" in 1983.

All In A Name

1. Johann Holzel was best known as what?

2. Who took their name from the "meaning of life" question in *The Hitchhiker's Guide To The Galaxy*?

3. Which English band took their name from a 1950 award-winning film starring Bette Davis.

4. Patrick Murray got his start with the (English) Beat on *Special Beat Service* - how is he best known?

5. This Body Snatchers off-shoot borrowed their name from a notorious female outlaw.

6. How is Dublin man Fionan Hanvey best known?

7. This Human League spin-off named themselves after a group in *A Clockwork Orange.*

8. This trio took their name from Hergé's famous *Tin Tin* cartoon.

9. Her real name is Myant Myant Aye but what is her stage name?

10. What is Buster Poindexter's real name?

Quiz #45

Vinyl Solutions

1. Their debut was *Lovely* and was a UK # 6 hit.

2. In 1986 *Flaunt It* was whose UK Top 10?

3. Whose *Blah Blah Blah* came out in 1986?

4. Their 1985 album *Night Time* was their highest charting UK hit.

5. *Saturday Night Sunday Morning* was which Glasgow duo's 1989 album?

6. *Sacred Heart* was a UK Top 10 in 1989 by who?

7. Who was *Cookin' On The Roof* in 1983?

8. *Floodland* was the 1987 UK hit from who?

9. Their album was *Too Much Pressure* in 1980.

10. Who simply called their 1986 release *Album* and *Cassette*?

Quiz #46

Bandstand

1. Who used to front Haircut 100?

2. Political man Peter Garrett was from which Australian Rock band?

3. David Byrne used to front this band.

4. Bernard Sumner and Johhny Marr united under what name?

5. Name Siouxie and Budgie's spin-off from the Banshees.

6. M People's Heather used to front this late '80s band.

7. Andy Partridge is from which English band?

8. Who founded The Teardrop Explodes before venturing off on his own in 1984?

9. Guy Chadwick fronted this English band.

10. Name The The's front man.

Quiz # 47

Celluloid & The Box

1. From *Electric Dreams*, "Together In Electric Dreams" was a near chart-topper for who?

2. "Eyes Of A Stranger" was featured on the *Valley Girl* sound-track - who sang it?

3. *American Gigolo* featured which # 1 Blondie track?

4. Who sang the US chart-topping single "St. Elmo's Fire (Man In Motion)"?

5. The Matthew Modine film *Vision Quest* featured which massive Madonna hit?

6. "I Do What I Do...(Theme For 9 & 1/2 Weeks)" was a US Top 40 hit by who?

7. Name the Scottish Pop-star who was in the film *Gregory's Girl.*

8. The festive film *Scrooged* featured whose "Put A Little Love In Your Heart"?

9. The film *Something Wild* featured his "Man With A Gun" single.

10. Which Ohio band sang the theme to the TV show *Square Pegs*?

Flashback Favourites

1. Which Pop-Goth band sang the 1985 single "Happy Boy"?

2. Who sang the hit single "Rapper's Delight"?

3. The single "Spiritwalker" was a UK Indie chart-topper for who?

4. Who was "Living On Video" in 1985?

5. "Everyday (Is Halloween)" was the seasonal track by who?

6. Which band asked "Why Me?" in 1983?

7. This San Francisco Punk band sang "Holiday In Cambodia".

8. "Let It Whip" was a US hit for who?

9. Who sang "Make A Circuit With Me"?

10. "Say It Again" was a club hit by which English outfit?

Quiz #49

Vinyl Solutions

1. Whose debut album was *Let Love Rule* in 1989?

2. In 1986 they had a UK hit record with *No. 10 Upping Street.*

3. The album *Bedrock Vice* was a 1987 release from who?

4. *Upstairs At Eric's* and *You And Me Both* were UK hits by who?

5. Which band's only success was with *New Clear Days* in 1980?

6. Who topped the UK chart with *It's Better To Travel* in 1987?

7. *Wild Child* was the first full-length release from which American Ska band?

8. *Sulk* was their 1987 album and biggest UK hit.

9. The follow-up to *Wonderful Life* was whose 1988 album *Comedy*?

10. Who released *Radical Departure* after the split of General Public?

Quiz #50

Single-Minded

1. Whose biggest UK hit was a cover of "Dear Prudence"?

2. This Ohio band sang the 1980 hit "Whip It".

3. Whose first hit "Sonic Boom Boy" was their biggest?

4. Which quartet sang the 1981 hit single "Once In A Lifetime"?

5. "Kiss This Thing Goodbye" was their only UK hit in the '80s.

6. Who drove "Fast Car" up the charts?

7. "Painted Moon" was their 1988 single.

8. Who sang "Goody Two Shoes"?

9. They released "Me Myself And I" in 1989.

10. Who had early '80s hits with "Poison Arrow" and "The Look Of Love"?

Quiz #51

Bandstand

1. Which '80s band would you associate with Kevin Rowland?

2. After being in a Dexy's off-shoot, Mick Talbot went on to be half of which British Pop duo?

3. Prior to Cracker, David Lowery fronted this Northern California band.

4. Mark Shaw used to front which London band?

5. Bobby Gillespie left Jesus & Mary Chain to start up which band?

6. Colin Newman was the founding member of which band?

7. Name the Polish singer who sang with Matt Bianco.

8. Natalie Merchant was in this Jamestown band in the '80s.

9. This '90s star got her break by singing on the 1989 Tears For Fears album *Seeds Of Love*.

10. Dan Baird was the lead vocalist of which Southern band?

Celluloid & The Box

1. Whose hit "Kiss And Tell" was featured in the Michael J. Fox film *Bright Lights Big City*?

2. The "Miami Vice" soundtrack featured their latin-titled "In Dulce Decorum" single.

3. Their cover of the Doors' "People Are Strange" was taken from the film *The Lost Boys.*

4. Which former Squeeze member was a presenter on the British television show "The Tube"?

5. He did the music for *Purple Rain* and topped the UK charts with his score for *Batman* in 1989.

6. Whose single "Gone Ridin" was in the film *American Flyers*?

7. Which British actor released the 1987 single "Generation Of Loneliness"?

8. Who recorded "Don't Box Me In" for the *Rumble Fish* soundtrack?

9. In 1986 who released the title track to the Tom Hanks/Jackie Gleeson film *Nothing In Common*?

10. The Yahoo Serious film *Young Einstein* featured their single "Great Southern Land".

Potluck

1. Name two bands that Vince Clarke has been a member of.

2. Who co-wrote "China Girl"?

3. They sang "Like Princes Do" in 1989.

4. Name Rob Fisher's band prior to Climie Fisher.

5. Who sang "Some Like It Hot" in 1985?

6. It was first the title of a 1958 book, then a 1981 Jam single and finally in 1986, a film - name it.

7. How is John Maher best known?

8. On what 1987 hit did Kirsty MacColl team up with the Pogues?

9. Before Crowded House, Tim Finn and brother Neil were together in which band?

10. Name two of the bands that Terry Hall has been in.

Single-Minded

1. Who sang the classics "What I Like About You" and "Talking In Your Sleep"?

2. "Just Like Heaven" was a US Top 40 for them in 1988.

3. "Don't Go" was their biggest UK hit.

4. Who had "Bette Davis Eyes" in 1981?

5. They had a UK hit with "The Harder I Try" in 1988.

6. Who followed up their "Lifeline" with "Communication" in 1983?

7. "Happy Ever After" was the optimistic debut from who?

8. Who had a huge hit with a cover of "Spirit In The Sky"?

9. "Respectable" was their chart-topping single in the UK.

10. Who teamed up with the Beatmasters for the 1989 UK Top 10 hit "I Can't Dance To That Music You're Playing"?

Quiz #55

Vinyl Solutions

1. "Motortown" was a hit from which 1987 Kane Gang album?

2. *Cupid & Pysche 85* was their aptly-titled 1985 release.

3. Whose US version was *Two Wheels Good* but in the UK was called *Steve McQueen*?

4. "Saved By Zero" and "One Thing Leads To Another" can be found on this Fixx album.

5. Whose first UK hit album was called *Soul Mining*?

6. This Rockabilly band was *Built For Speed* in 1982.

7. Who released *Virgins & Philistines* in 1985?

8. *Night And Day* was the 1982 hit by who?

9. Their 1985 album was the *Seventh Dream Of A Teenage Heaven.*

10. Whose debut album *The White Room* was released in 1989 but not a hit until 1991?

Flashback Favourites

1. Who sang "Never Never" in 1983?

2. Miles Copeland managed this Gothic band whose tracks included "Dance With Me" and "Open Your Eyes".

3. Which American Punk band sang "Lady Killer" in the early '80s?

4. Who was "Living On The Ceiling" in 1982?

5. "Life Is Life" was a Euro-disco hit for them in 1987.

6. "Another Generation" and "Party At Ground Zero" are songs by which Californian Ska band?

7. Who sang "World Destruction" in 1985?

8. "Don't Crash The Car Tonight" was their 1989 track.

9. Who released "Acceleration" in 1984?

10. Which Los Angeles band is responsible for the patriotic track "4th Of July"?

Wonders Of The World

1. Who was "The Rain" a hit for in 1986?

2. "Love Changes (Everything)" was their only US hit.

3. Their only UK hit was "Safety Dance" in 1983.

4. Annie Lennox had a huge hit with "No More 'I Love You's" - who had a UK hit with it in the '80s?

5. "Waiting For A Star To Fall" was their UK hit in 1988.

6. Whose "Scatterlings Of Africa" was a UK hit in 1983?

7. They sang "Are You Sure?" in 1988.

8. "Somebody's Watching Me" was the UK hit for who?

9. Madonna was a one-time member of this band who sang "Right On Track".

10. "Live It Up" was this Australian band's only UK success.

US # 1 Albums

1. Whose *Sports* and *Fore!* albums both spent a week on top of the US charts?

2. *The Raw & The Cooked* was the US # 1 for which English trio?

3. Whose *Songs From The Big Chair* topped the US charts?

4. Her *Promise* album topped both the US and UK charts in 1985.

5. *Make It Big* did just that for who in 1984?

6. Whose *Licensed To Ill* went to # 1 in 1986?

7. *Beauty & The Beat* was their chart-topping debut in 1981.

8. Whose debut *Business As Usual* was a chart-topper?

9. *Synchronicity* was their only chart-topping album in the US.

10. Mr. Mister's "Broken Wings" and "Kyrie" can be found on which # 1 album?

Quiz #59

Vinyl Solutions

1. *Escapade* was his debut solo album in 1983.

2. *Porcupine* and *Crocodiles* are two albums from which Liverpool band?

3. *The Thin Red Line* was whose 1986 US hit album?

4. *Beauty Stab* and *How To Be A Zillionaire* were UK hits from who?

5. Who had a hit in 1988 with *Diesel & Dust*?

6. Suzanne Vega was featured on whose 1989 album *Steady On*?

7. Whose 1984 album was *Points On The Curve*?

8. *The People Who Grinned Themselves To Death* was their second album.

9. Which Welsh band had a UK Top 40 hit with *Discover* in 1987?

10. *Mars Needs Guitars!* and *Stoneage Romeos* were early releases from which Australian outfit?

All In A Name

1. This popular duo took their name from a "sale" sign in a furniture shop in Hull.

2. Who is Sally Daillon?

3. Who was the inspiration behind both Frankie Goes To Hollywood and Danny Wilson's names?

4. How is Bruce Robert Howard better known?

5. Which all-girl Scottish band borrowed their name from a 1961 Elvis single?

6. The 1964 film *The Dream Syndicate* was the inspiration behind which English band's name?

7. How is John Mellors better known?

8. Douglas Trendle is the larger than life frontman of Bad Manners - how is he best known?

9. They took their name from a character in the Jane Fonda film *Barbarella*.

10. How do James Osterburg's fans refer to him?

Quiz #61

Single-Minded

1. They sang "Lifeboat Party" and "Endicott".

2. Who sang "I Ran (So Far Away)" and "Wishing (I Had A Photograph Of You)"?

3. Whose first UK hit was the Einstein-inspired "$E=mc^2$"?

4. Who followed up his debut UK chart-topper with another one called "Cars"?

5. Who was "Walking On Sunshine" in 1985?

6. His ode to working-life was "5 O'Clock World".

7. Who sang the 1989 single "(What's Wrong With) Dreaming"?

8. She nearly topped the UK charts in 1979 with "Lucky Number".

9. In 1982 who released the US Top 40 hit "Valley Girl"?

10. Their "Love Like Blood" was a 1985 UK hit.

Bandstand

1. Who sang back up for Adam & The Ants and Dexy's Midnight Runners before releasing "Stop"?

2. This Undertones off-shoot featured the O'Neill brothers and American Steve Mack on vocals.

3. Midge Ure and some Magazine men formed which Synth band?

4. This Liverpool band featured the likes of Holly Johnson, Bill Drummond, Ian Broudie and Budgie.

5. In 1986 the line up for which band was Paul Heaton, Stan Cullimore, Norman Cook and Hugh Whitaker?

6. Keren, Sarah and Siobhan formed which trio in 1980?

7. Which Dublin band featured Gavin Friday and Kik Evans (The Edge's brother)?

8. Swiss men Dieter Meier and Boris Blank were known as what?

9. Carol Decker fronted this '80s band.

10. Which band featured Stewart Copeland, Stanley Clarke and Deborah Holland on vocals?

Quiz #63

Vinyl Solutions

1. Who followed up their *Japanese Whispers* with *The Top* in 1984?

2. *Dream Into Action* and *One To One* were both UK Top 10 albums for who?

3. Their *Broadcast* album was a US hit in 1987.

4. *F.L.M.* was a Top 5 album in the UK for which duo?

5. Which band released *Correct Use Of Soap* in 1980?

6. His debut solo album was *Deep In The Heart Of Nowhere*.

7. *Running In The Family* and *Staring At The Sun* were consecutive UK # 2 albums for who?

8. Whose first UK hit album was *Entertainment* in 1979?

9. Their album *Bummed* was released at the end of 1989.

10. Her UK Top 10 was *So Good* in 1988.

Flashback Favourites

1. Who sang "Russian Radio" at the end of the '80s?

2. "The Lunatics (Have Taken Over The Asylum)" was the debut UK hit for who?

3. They sang "Everywhere I Go" and "Let The Day Begin".

4. In 1983 who sang "Kiss Kiss Bang Bang"?

5. "Da Da Da" nearly topped the UK charts for this German band.

6. Who was "Thinking Of You" in 1985?

7. Which Talking Heads spin-off had a hit with "Genius Of Love"?

8. Who sang "Down Under"?

9. "People Who Died" was a single by who in 1981?

10. Who sang "88 Lines (About 44 Women)"?

Quiz #65

Single-Minded

1. These Texans sang the single "The Future's So Bright I Gotta Wear Shades".

2. "She Sells Sanctuary" was a 1985 single by who?

3. Who was "So Lonely" in 1980?

4. Whose first of two US hits was "Kids In America" in 1982?

5. Whose first UK Top 40 single was "The Rattler"?

6. Who sang the 1987 hit "Luka"?

7. "The King of Rock 'n' Roll" was their 1988 hit.

8. "Promised You A Miracle" was the first UK Top 20 for who?

9. In 1984 this Melbourne band had a US Top 40 hit "Send Me An Angel".

10. It was second time lucky for whose UK hit "Mary's Prayer"?

Quiz #66

Bandstand

1. Before the Bad Seeds, Nick Cave was in which festively-named band?

2. At the front of which band would you find Edwyn Collins?

3. Ian McCulloch was the leader of this band.

4. This Edinburgh man used to front Josef K.

5. Martin Fry fronted which Pop outfit?

6. Chris Stamey and Peter Holsapple were in which New York band?

7. Members of the early '80s Synth-band Freur resurfaced as what?

8. Steve Kilbey used to front which Australian band?

9. Which band featured Morten Harket?

10. Black Grape's Shaun Ryder was a founding member of what band in 1980?

Quiz #67

Vinyl Solutions

1. *Freedom Of Choice* was this Ohio band's US Top 40 hit in 1980.

2. They followed up their self-titled debut with *Listen* in 1983.

3. Which LA quintet followed up *All Four One* with *Little Robbers* in 1983?

4. Name the former Buzzcock who released *Jerky Versions Of The Dream*.

5. Who were *Shooting Rubberbands At The Stars* in 1989?

6. Which band had only one UK hit *Big Bang* in 1989?

7. Who was *Dancing On The Couch* in 1987?

8. The British release of their debut was called *Theodore & Friends* whilst in the US it was self-titled.

9. Who released *Bête Noire* in 1987?

10. *The Twelve Commandments Of Dance* almost topped the UK charts for who?

Quiz #68

Single-Minded

1. In 1982 who sang the US hit "We Got The Beat"?

2. Who debuted with "Perfect Skin" in 1984?

3. "Pass The Dutchie" was a big hit by who?

4. Who took "Tour De France" into the UK charts two Summers in a row?

5. "People Are People" was their only US hit in the '80s.

6. Who sang "Digging Your Scene" in 1986?

7. "Ghost Town" was a UK chart-topping hit by who?

8. Who was "Driving Away From Home" in the Spring of '86?

9. "Electric Avenue" nearly topped the US charts for who?

10. Who was "Oblivious" in 1983?

Quiz #69

Wonders Of The World

1. They sang “Whirly Girl” in 1983.

2. “The Politics Of Dancing” was a hit by who?

3. Name the Australian band that took “Holiday” to the Top 30 in the US.

4. “I Don’t Mind At All” was this band’s 1987 US hit.

5. Whose US hit was entitled “I Eat Cannibals”?

6. Name the band and song whose only US hit was the very first video ever to be played on MTV.

7. She choreographed *American Graffitti* and had a # 1 with “Micky” in 1982.

8. This Californian band’s only US hit was “Welcome To The Boomtown”.

9. In 1988 this German band was “Keeping The Dream Alive”.

10. Their “Nellie The Elephant” was a UK Top 5 in 1984.

Bandstand

1. Clark Datchler used to front which British Pop band?

2. Scotsman Roddy Frame fronted this Scottish band.

3. Paddy McAloon formed what band in 1982?

4. Chris Hamill (aka Limahl) was the frontman of which band?

5. Name either one of Kirk Brandon's bands.

6. Name Tracy Thorn's band prior to Everything But The Girl.

7. Pete Wylie used to front this Liverpool band.

8. Luther Campbell formed this controversial Rap band in 1985.

9. Wendy James was a co-founder of which English band?

10. Name the Wham! and Style Council back up singer who married Paul Weller in 1986.

Quiz #71

Vinyl Solutions

1. *Tropical Gangsters* and *Doppleganger* were UK Top 40 albums by who?

2. Whose most successful album was *Phantasmagoria*?

3. *Shabooh Shoobah* and *Listen Like Thieves* were albums by who?

4. In 1984 *The Age Of Consent* was their debut hit album.

5. Whose *Watermark* album was a UK # 5?

6. Their debut *Shakespeare Alabama* was a UK Top 40 for who?

7. In 1983 their *Touch* album went to # 1 in the UK.

8. The UK Top 40 album *Good Deeds And Dirty Rags* was whose 1989 debut?

9. In 1985 who released the UK Top 10 album *Flaunt The Imperfection*?

10. Who followed up his chart-topping debut with *Neither Fish Nor Flesh*?

Quiz #72

Celluloid & The Box

1. Which Gothic band had a cameo performance in David Bowie's *The Hunger*?

2. *True Stories* was the name of their film and album in 1986.

3. In 1988 which band released "Doctorin' The Tardis" a tribute to the cult TV show "Dr Who"?

4. *Do The Right Thing* featured whose "Fight The Power"?

5. In 1980 the film *Rude Boy* featured this band.

6. The American Sitcom "Get A Life" had this band's "Stand" as the theme song.

7. This trio featured members of the Beat and took their name from a 1960 MGM film.

8. Which Welsh band took their name from a TV show in Britain and debuted with *Pop Said*?

9. A "Star Trek" Vulcan princess was the inspiration for their name.

10. Who played the character May Day in the James Bond film *A View To A Kill*?

Quiz #73

Single-Minded

1. Who sang "Underneath The Radar"?

2. Which band featured the computer-generated Max Headroom on their "Paranoimia" single?

3. "Sunglasses At Night" was whose 1984 US Top 10?

4. "Stand By" and "Don't Try To Stop It" were 1983 singles by who?

5. Who sang the chart-topping hit "Rock Me Amadeus" in 1986?

6. Which English band sang "Martha's Harbour"?

7. "She Bangs The Drums" was the first UK hit by who?

8. Who had a US # 1 with "Toy Soldiers" in 1989?

9. "Everyday Is Like Sunday" was the follow-up to whose "Suedehead"?

10. Who released the 1981 UK Top 5 hits "Souvenir" and "Joan Of Arc"?

Quiz #74

Bandstand

1. Martha Davis was the leader of this LA band.

2. Hugh Cornwell was the lead singer in which band?

3. Boo Hewerdine was the lead singer in which Cambridge-based band?

4. What is the name of Robert Smith's band?

5. This Californian band featured Exene Cervenka and John Doe.

6. Sinead O'Connor was briefly a member of which band?

7. Mancrab was an off-shoot of which English outfit?

8. Johnette Napolitano fronted which Los Angeles Rock band?

9. In the late '70s and early '80s, Pete Shelley was in which Punk band?

10. Name the popular duo that were once back up singers for Wham?

Quiz #75

Flashback Favourites

1. He released a single called "Vertigo" in 1989.

2. Who had a "Mirror In The Bathroom" in 1980?

3. "Never Say Never" and "A Girl In Trouble" were singles from which San Francisco band?

4. They had moderate success with "Eardrum Buzz" in the Spring of '89.

5. Which Cleveland band was "Waiting For Mary" in 1989?

6. In 1986 this band released "One Simple Thing".

7. Who sang "China" in 1983?

8. "Wordy Rappinghood" was a 1981 UK hit from who?

9. "Everywhere That I'm Not" and "No Time Like Now" are tracks by which Californian band?

10. In 1986 whose "Suzi's On The Ball Now" single was produced by Ian Broudie?

Quiz #76

Potluck

1. U2's The Edge teamed up with who to release "Heroine (Theme From Captive)"?

2. Prior to his stint as an MTV Europe VJ, what band was Miles Hunt in?

3. Which prestigious label was the early home to the likes of Edwyn Collins and Aztec Camera?

4. Name the two bands you associate with Jimmy Somerville.

5. Band Aid's "Do They Know It's Christmas" went straight to # 1 in the UK - who wrote it?

6. The Hothouse Flowers helped out on whose "Closer To Fine" single?

7. There were two versions of this Peter Gabriel song - one was sung in German.

8. Which 1979 album did *Rolling Stone* critics deem the "Album Of The '80s"?

9. *World Shut Your Mouth* was whose UK Top 40 solo album and single?

10. Members of UB40, Madness and General Public got together to record which 1985 Ethopian famine-relief single?

Quiz #77

Vinyl Solutions

1. In 1979 who released *Valley Of The Dolls*?

2. Which Finnish rockers had a UK Top 40 album with *Two Steps From the Move*?

3. Whose *The Big Lad In The Windmill* was their most successful album?

4. In 1988 their album *Little Children* nearly topped the UK charts.

5. *Darklands* and *Barbed Wire Kisses* were UK Top 10 albums for who?

6. Whose *A Word To The Wise Guy* was a 1984 UK Top 30 album?

7. *If I Should Fall From Grace With God* was a Top 5 hit in the UK for who?

8. In 1980 who had *Seconds Of Pleasure* with a UK Top 30 album?

9. Which outfit was *Hypnotised* with their UK Top 10 album in 1980?

10. Whose UK hit album was *Sold* in 1987?

Single-Minded

1. Their first hit single was "Tell That Girl To Shut Up".

2. In 1985 they released "I Thought I'd Never See You Again" and "Sweet Nothing".

3. They released the UK hit "Respect Yourself" in 1984.

4. "I Don't Want A Lover" was whose debut single?

5. Their "Give A Little Love" nearly topped the UK chart.

6. Who released "Return To Yesterday" in 1988?

7. Whose "Sit Down" was first released in the Summer of '89?

8. "There's A Ghost In My House" was a UK Top 30 in 1987 for who?

9. Who sang "I Know What Boys Like" in 1982?

10. "Sweetest Smile" was whose UK Top 10?

Quiz #79

US # 1 Singles

1. Which London-based band sang “Wild Wild West” in 1988?

2. The Bangles had two chart-toppers - name either one.

3. Whose cover of the Hall & Oates’ hit “Everytime You Go Away” was a chart-topper?

4. Formerly the leader of the Baby’s, who sang “Missing You”?

5. U2 had two US chart-topping hits in the ‘80s - name either one.

6. Which Australian sang “Jessie’s Girl” in 1981?

7. Who topped the US charts with a cover of “You Keep Me Hanging On”?

8. Shocking Blue topped the US charts with “Venus” in 1969 - who did the same with it in 1986?

9. “(I Just) Died In Your Arms” was whose # 1 hit?

10. The first two US hits by Tears For Fears topped the charts - name either one.

Quiz #80

Bandstand

1. Dukes of Stratosphear was an alter ego of which English band?

2. Mike Edwards formed which band in 1988?

3. Which English group features Harriet Wheeler's vocals?

4. Roland Gift was the lead singer of which band?

5. In which Dublin band would you find Liam O'Maonlai?

6. Graham Skinner and Pim Jones were founding members of which Glasgow Pop band?

7. Which influential band did Chuck Prophet join in 1984?

8. Gary Daly and Eddie Lundon formed which band in Merseyside in 1979?

9. Which trio featured Ian Marsh, Martyn Ware and Glenn Gregory on vocals?

10. Raintree Crow features some original members of which '80s band?

Quiz #81

Vinyl Solutions

1. *Pleasure Victim* was the US debut for who?

2. Who went to # 2 in the UK with *Too Rye Aye*?

3. *New York* was whose biggest UK hit from the '80s?

4. Whose only UK hit was *Laughing At The Pieces*?

5. *Angst In My Pants* was this Californian band's 1982 album.

6. They followed up their self-titled debut with *Gatecrashing* in 1989.

7. Whose 1986 album was *Animal Magic*?

8. In 1980 who was *Flogging A Dead Horse*?

9. Their album *Like Gangbusters* went Top 20 in the UK in 1983.

10. All of their albums were UK Top 10 hits, and in 1980 it was *Vienna*.

Potluck

1. "Kiss Me" was the 1985 UK Top 5 from who?

2. In Tommy Tutone's song, what was Jenny's telephone number?

3. "She Blinded Me With Science" was whose only US hit?

4. Who sang the 1988 UK hit single "Joe Le Taxi"?

5. "Wheels Of Wonder" and "Healing At The Harbour" were 1989 singles by which Glasgow Rock band?

6. Klark Kent was the alter ego of who?

7. They followed up their debut US hit single "And We Danced" with 1986's "Day By Day".

8. Who sang the 1979 UK hit "Are Friends Electric"?

9. Which 1985 Smiths' hit did Soho sample for their 1990 hit "Hippy Chick"?

10. Who sang "I Melt With You"?

Quiz #83

Flashback Favourites

1. Who sang the UK Top 40 hit "Free Yourself"?

2. They sang "Numbers With Wings" and "Barbarella".

3. "Biting My Nails" was a single by who?

4. "I Touch Roses" and "Boy" were singles by which Los Angeles band?

5. This band sang "Eighties" in 1984.

6. This Fall off-shoot were "Waking Up In The Sun" in 1989.

7. Who had a US hit in 1983 with "Twilight Zone"?

8. "Don't Sniff Coke" was a single by who?

9. Who released the raunchy dance club hit "Tastes So Good" in 1984?

10. "Independence Day" was a single from which Sheffield band?

Quiz #84

Singled-Minded

1. Whose first UK hit single was "Song For Whoever"?

2. "Heaven (Must Be There)" and "Can't Wait To See You" are singles from which Australian band?

3. "Chuck E's In Love" was a hit in both the US and UK for who?

4. "When Will I Be Famous?" was their 1988 UK # 1.

5. Whose first US hit was "Do You Believe In Love"?

6. "I Got You" was the 1980 UK hit by who?

7. Who took "One Step Beyond" into the UK charts in 1979?

8. Whose UK debut hit was called "Wishing I Was Lucky"?

9. "Yeah Yeah Yeah Yeah Yeah" was a 1988 single by who?

10. Whose UK debut was the Top 10 single "My One Temptation"?

Quiz #85

Bandstand

1. Colin Vearncombe was the core member of this Liverpool band.

2. Singer Mike Peters fronted this Welsh Rock band.

3. Bob Mould founded which band in 1979?

4. Susanna Hoffs was in which band?

5. Who was the Television frontman that released "A Town Called Walker" in 1987?

6. Dali's Car consisted of who?

7. Johnny McElhone of Texas got his start in which Scottish Pop band?

8. Michael Hutchence was the lead singer of which Australian band?

9. Name the legendary outfit that was co-founded by Joe Strummer.

10. Gary Clark was from which Scottish band?

UK # 1 Albums

1. *Sparkle In The Rain* was the first of four consecutive UK chart-toppers for who?

2. *Never For Ever* was whose UK # 1?

3. *Colour By Numbers* was the only chart-topping hit for who?

4. Their debut *Lexicon Of Love* was whose chart-topper?

5. *Eat To The Beat* was whose UK # 1 album in 1979?

6. *When The World Knows Your Name* was this Glasgow band's chart-topping second release.

7. In 1987 *Keep Your Distance* was a chart-topping hit for this London quartet.

8. Whose 1980 album was *Kings Of The Wild Frontier*?

9. Their only chart-topping UK album was *Steeltown* in 1984.

10. *The Innocents* and *Wild!* both topped the UK chart for who?

Single-Minded

1. Who had a big hit with their "Hands To Heaven" in 1988?

2. "Alone Without You" was a UK Top 10 in 1985 for who?

3. They sang "Graceland" in 1989.

4. "Shiny Shiny" was their 1983 UK hit.

5. Who sang "Here Comes Your Man" in 1989?

6. In 1983 "(Keep Feeling) Fascination" was a massive hit for them.

7. Whose debut was the UK smash hit "Love Missile F1-11"?

8. Who had the UK Top 5 "Sign Of The Times" in 1983?

9. "Walking In L.A." and "Destination Unknown" were tracks by who?

10. Who sang the classic track "Blue Monday"?

Potluck

1. Henry Rollins left which seminal punk band in 1986 to embark on a solo career?

2. Who got together to record "Change Your Mind" in 1985?

3. This Scottish band sang "The Whole Of The Moon" in 1985.

4. Who sang "I Want You Back" in 1983?

5. The film *The Krays* starred the Kemp brothers - name their '80s band.

6. Who had a hit with "Our Lips Are Sealed"?

7. They collaborated on "Don't Give Up".

8. Who is Robert Fripp's famous wife?

9. Dusty Springfield helped out on their single "What Have I Done To Deserve This?".

10. They sang the UK Top 10 hits "Heaven Knows I'm Miserable Now" and "Sheila Take A Bow".

Quiz #89

Vinyl Solutions

1. *Wha'appen* was whose follow-up to *I Just Can't Stop It*?

2. In 1986 their *Victorialand* was a UK Top 10.

3. Whose *Stuck In Wonderamaland* came out in 1989?

4. They released *The Eight Legged Groove Machine* in 1988.

5. In 1989 who released their greatest hits album *Pastpresent*?

6. Who released the 1984 UK Top 40 album *Heaven Is Waiting*?

7. *Raw Like Sushi* was a UK # 2 for who?

8. *The Ups And Downs* was whose UK Top 40 album in 1985?

9. *Rattlesnakes* was the 1984 debut from who?

10. Who released *Whammy!* in 1983?

Quiz #90

Under-Cover

1. They had a UK Top 5 with a funky version of "Money".

2. This band sampled "New Years Day" on their "A Bif Of..." single.

3. Who had a UK hit with their version of "I Want Candy"?

4. Their cover of "Ball Of Confusion" was a dance club hit.

5. Whose "Always Something There To Remind Me" was a US Top 10 hit in 1983?

6. Who had a UK Top 5 hit with a cover of "Wild World" in 1988?

7. Name the gothic band who did a zany version of "Like A Virgin".

8. This band had a hit with Neil Diamond's "Red Red Wine".

9. Name the Glasgow duo who covered Kate Bush's "Man With A Child In His Eyes".

10. Who had a UK # 1 in '81 with their cover of "Tainted Love"?

Answers

Vinyl Solutions

1. Their only US hit was the 1982 album *Non-Stop Erotic Cabaret.*
   Soft Cell

2. Which Scottish band released the UK Top 5 *Southside* in 1989?
   Texas

3. Who released the *Conscious Party* in 1988?
   Ziggy Marley & The Melody Makers

4. *Picture Book* was whose debut hit album?
   Simply Red

5. *The Youth Of Today* was their 1983 album.
   Musical Youth

6. Which quartet released *Stop Making Sense* in 1984?
   Talking Heads

7. Who followed up their self-titled debut with *Talk Talk Talk?*
   Psychedelic Furs

8. *Once Upon A Time* was a US Top 10 for them.
   Simple Minds

9. Their 1984 album was simply called *Pop.*
   Tones On Tail

10. Who released *The Colour Of Spring* in the Spring of '86?
    Talk Talk

Flashback Favourites

1. "Birds Fly (Whisper To A Scream)" was whose 1984 single?
   Icicle Works

2. Which former member of Magazine recorded the ethereal "Rainy Season"?
   Howard Devoto

3. Name the band that sang "Hand On My Heart" in 1984.
   Shriekback

4. Who sang "Swear" in 1983?
   Tim Scott

5. They sang "AEIOU Sometimes Y" in 1984.
   EBN-OZN

6. "Chamber Of Hellos" and "I'll Do You" were college radio classics by which Californian band?
   Wire Train

7. In 1988, which Dublin band sang "Call Me Blue"?
   A House

8. Whose 1987 sad tale was entitled "Hope Road"?
   Anne Clark

9. "Baby's In The Mountains" was a single from who in 1983?
   Peter Godwin

10. In 1984 Robert Görl of DAF released "Darling Don't Leave Me" - which cropped-haired songstress helped on vocals?
    Annie Lennox

Single-Minded

1. Who sang "Like An Animal" in 1983?
   The Glove

2. They followed their US hit "Voices Carry" with another "What About Love" in 1986.
   Til Tuesday

3. Whose first US hit was "Keep On Movin"?
   Soul II Soul

4. What was the name of Public Image Limited's anti-love hit in 1983?
   "This Is Not A Love Song"

5. Their "I Wanna Be A Flintstone" had international appeal in 1988.
   Screaming Blue Messiahs

6. The biggest UK hit for them was "The Word Girl" in 1985.
   Scritti Politti

7. Whose "Relax" was in the UK chart for four months?
   Frankie Goes To Hollywood

8. Twice they had a UK Top 20 hit with "Love Will Tear Us Apart".
   Joy Division

9. Who sang "I Don't Want To Be A Hero" and "Shattered Dreams"?
   Johnny Hates Jazz

10. "My Ever Changing Moods" was their only US hit.
    The Style Council

Potluck

1. Who took *The Road To Hell* to the top of the UK charts in 1989?
   Chris Rea

2. In 1987 these former members of Japan released a single called "Buoy".
   Mick Karn with David Sylvian

3. Simply Red topped the US charts twice in the '80s - name either track.
   "Holding Back The Years" or "If You Don't Know Me By Now"

4. *La Bamba* was the name of whose US chart-topping album and single?
   Los Lobos

5. Whose name is derived from the phrase "kiss my ass" in Gaelic?
   The Pogues

6. At one time, this New Romantic band featured Stephen "Tin Tin" Duffy.
   Duran Duran

7. Which Austrian band featured their name in the title of their 1989 UK Top 5 hit?
   Edelweiss ("Bring Me Edelweiss")

8. John Lennon said they were his favourite band in 1980.
   The B-52's

9. Both the Eurythmics and Madonna had a single with the same title, in '83 and '87 respectively - what is it?
   "Who's That Girl?"

10. Who worked with the Gang Of Four and Alison Moyet before starting Fairground Attraction?
    Eddi Reader

Vinyl Solutions

1. *The Lion And The Cobra* was the debut from who?
   Sinead O'Connor

2. "Favourite Shirts" and "Love Plus One" were hit singles from which Haircut 100 album?
   Pelican West

3. Name the Californian band who released *Mother's Milk* in 1989.
   Red Hot Chili Peppers

4. Who had a UK hit in 1983 with *Deep Sea Skiving*?
   Bananarama

5. *Outlandos D'Amour* and *Reggatta De Blanc* were hit albums from which British trio?
   The Police

6. Whose debut album was *The Crossing*?
   Big Country

7. *Kissing To Be Clever* and *Waking Up With The House On Fire* were hit albums from who?
   Culture Club

8. Who was *Hunting High & Low* in 1985?
   A-Ha

9. Their 1985 album was ...*All The Rage.*
   General Public

10. Whose early releases included *Construction Time Again* and *Speak And Spell*?
    Depêche Mode

Bandstand

1. Debbie Harry used to front which American band?
   Blondie

2. Alison Moyet and Vince Clarke were known as what?
   Yazoo (aka Yaz)

3. Name the Los Angeles band that featured Peter Case.
   The Plimsouls

4. What is the name of the band Peter Murphy fronted in the '80s?
   Bauhaus

5. Maria McKee was the lead woman in this '80s band.
   Lone Justice

6. Feargal Sharkey was in which Irish band?
   The Undertones

7. Porno For Pyro's Perry Farrell was the founding member of which '80s band?
   Jane's Addiction

8. Tom Bailey, Alannah Currie and Joe Leeway were known as what?
   The Thompson Twins

9. David Baerwald and David Ricketts made up which Los Angeles Rock duo?
   David & David

10. What Scottish band was Karl Wallinger a member of before World Party?
    The Waterboys

Single-Minded

1. Who sang "Since Yesterday" in 1984?
   Strawberry Switchblade

2. "Tomorrow People" was their first UK hit.
   Ziggy Marley & The Melody Makers

3. "Rock Lobster" and "Private Idaho" are classic tracks by who?
   The B-52's

4. Which New Romantic band sang "We Came To Dance" and "Dancing With Tears In My Eyes"?
   Ultravox

5. "Candybar Express" was the first UK hit for which Glasgow Pop band?
   Love & Money

6. They were "Calling All The Heroes" in 1986.
   It Bites!

7. Who was "Close (To The Edit)" in 1984?
   Art Of Noise

8. "Mexican Radio" was their 1983 UK hit.
   Wall Of Voodoo

9. They had UK # 2 hits with both "Cool For Cats" and "Up The Junction".
   Squeeze

10. Who was "Making Plans For Nigel" in 1979?
    XTC

Celluloid & The Box

1. Who did the title track to the film *Never Ending Story*?
   Limahl

2. In 1989 their US Top 10 "Room To Move" was featured in *My Stepmother's An Alien*.
   Animotion

3. Whose hit "Romancing The Stone" wasn't actually in the film?
   Eddy Grant

4. She appeared in *Valley Girl* performing her 1982 single "Johnny Are You Queer?".
   Josie Cotton

5. Whose "Buffalo Stance" was featured in the film *Slaves Of New York*?
   Neneh Cherry

6. In 1985 they topped the US charts with the title song to *A View To A Kill.*
   Duran Duran

7. The film *Howard The Duck* featured whose music?
   Thomas Dolby

8. Which band did the soundtrack to the film *To Live And Die In LA*?
   Wang Chung

9. *Nuns On The Run* is a film that featured whose UK Top 10 hit "The Race"?
   Yello

10. They did the title track to the film *The Living Daylights* in 1987.
    A-Ha

Vinyl Solutions

1. Whose 1986 compilation was called *Street Life 20 Great Hits*?
   Roxy Music

2. Her debut *Ancient Heart* was a UK # 3.
   Tanita Tikaram

3. Whose solo UK hit was the 1989 album *Read My Lips*?
   Jimmy Somerville

4. The 1987 album *Babble* was a UK Top 30 hit for who?
   That Petrol Emotion

5. *Brilliant Trees* was whose 1984 debut solo album?
   David Sylvian

6. Which Anglo-American band released *Let It Bee* in 1988?
   Voice Of The Beehive

7. Who had UK chart success with their 1988 *What Up Dog* album?
   Was (Not Was)

8. The 1985 album *World Service* was nearly a Top 10 hit in the UK for who?
   Spear Of Destiny

9. Whose 1981 US hit album was *The Completion Backward Principle*?
   The Tubes

10. *Sunshine On Leith* was whose UK Top 10 album?
    The Proclaimers

All In A Name

1. What is Elvis Costello's real name?
   Declan McManus

2. Which German Synth band took their name from a 1965 French sci-fi film?
   Alphaville

3. Frank Tovey's pseudonymn is what?
   Fad Gadget

4. Which Glasgow band's name is said to be Greek for "Into The Womb"?
   Del Amitri

5. How is Buzzcock Howard Trafford best known?
   Howard Devoto

6. This Irish band's name means "family" in Gaelic.
   Clannad

7. Which English band took their name from a Russian ballet company?
   The Bolshoi

8. Who is Hugh Cregg III?
   Huey Lewis

9. This Manchester band took their name from a rough area in Glasgow.
   Easterhouse

10. How is William Wolfe Broad best known?
    Billy Idol

Bandstand

1. Marc Almond and David Ball were known as what?
Soft Cell

2. Which Canadian band features siblings Margo, Michael and Peter Timmons?
Cowboy Junkies

3. This trio featured two guys named Paul and their debut *A Walk Across The Rooftops.*
Blue Nile

4. Difford & Tillbrook were members of which English Pop band?
Squeeze

5. This Brisbane band featured the talents of Grant McLennan and Robert Forster.
The Go Betweens

6. Which duo featured Neil Arthur and Steven Luscombe?
Blancmange

7. Thurston Moore and Kim Gordon were from which New York band?
Sonic Youth

8. Dave Wakeling and Rankin' Roger formed the core of General Public - what was their previous band?
The (English) Beat

9. This Welsh band featured twins Jay and Michael Aston.
Gene Loves Jezebel

10. Peter Zaremba was lead man in which New York Cult band?
The Fleshtones

Single-Minded

1. He sang the UK # 1 "Nineteen" in '85.
   Paul Hardcastle

2. In 1988 "Rok Da House" was a UK # 5 hit for who?
   Beatmasters (featuring Cookie Crew)

3. Their first UK Top 10 was "Happy Hour" in 1986.
   The Housemartins

4. In 1988 it was second time lucky with "Voyage Voyage" for this French vocalist.
   Desireless

5. "Don't Call Me Baby" was whose UK Top 20 single?
   Voice Of The Beehive

6. She was a "Slave To The Rhythm" in 1985.
   Grace Jones

7. Who followed up their chart-topping UK hit with "Come Back and Stay" in 1983?
   Paul Young

8. They sang "On My Radio" in 1979.
   Selector

9. Their second UK hit was "No Sleep Till Brooklyn" in 1987.
   Beastie Boys

10. Who released the 1987 UK hit "Stutter Rap (No Sleep Til Bedtime)"?
    Morris Minor & The Majors

Vinyl Solutions

1. Whose only UK hit album was *Shangri-La* in 1985?
   Animal Nightlife

2. In 1982 they released the UK Top 10 *Fabrique*.
   Fashion

3. *Punch The Clock* was the 1983 hit album from who?
   Elvis Costello

4. In 1984 who had the UK hit album *Sisters*?
   The Bluebells

5. *Dig The New Breed* was the follow-up to whose UK # 1 *The Gift*?
   The Jam

6. *Blue Sunshine* was their UK Top 20 hit in 1983.
   The Glove

7. Their only album was *Where The Action Is*.
   Westworld

8. Which British duo had a UK hit with *Everything* in 1988?
   Climie Fisher

9. *Oil On Canvas* was the only UK Top 10 album by who?
   Japan

10. Whose 1984 debut was the hit album *She's So Unusual*?
    Cyndi Lauper

Wonders Of The World

1. Whose only UK hit was "Big In Japan"?
   Alphaville

2. "Tantalise (Wo Wo Ee Yeh Yeh)" was the UK Top 20 hit for who in 1983?
   Jimmy The Hoover

3. Two one-hit wonders had hits with "Funky Town" (aka "Funkytown") - name either.
   Lipps Inc. or Pseudo Echo

4. Who had a hit with "Tarzan Boy" in 1985?
   Baltimora

5. In 1980 who sang "Echo Beach"?
   Martha & The Muffins

6. Whose only UK hit was "Obsession" in 1985?
   Animotion

7. This British duo had moderate success with "Shooting From My Heart".
   Big Bam Boo

8. Which Australian band's UK hit was "That's When I Think Of You".
   1927

9. "Pump Up The Volume" was a UK # 1 and their only hit.
   M/A/R/R/S

10. Whose cover of "Can't Help Falling In Love" was a 1986 UK hit?
    Lick The Tins

UK # 1 Albums

1. *Let's Dance* was one of the UK chart-toppers by who?
   David Bowie

2. Name the chart-topping Duran Duran album that featured the singles "The Reflex" and "Union Of The Snake".
   7 & The Ragged Tiger

3. *Welcome To The Pleasuredome* was a hit album for who in 1984?
   Frankie Goes To Hollywood

4. Their *Technique* topped the charts in 1989.
   New Order

5. What was the name of Peter Gabriel's # 1 album from 1986?
   So

6. Name the Smiths' chart-topping album from 1985.
   Meat Is Murder

7. *Boys & Girls* was the 1985 chart-topper for who?
   Bryan Ferry

8. Who released the hit album *Dare* in 1981?
   Human League

9. Whose *Legend* was a chart-topper in 1984?
   Bob Marley & The Wailers

10. *Nothing Like The Sun* was the only UK # 1 in the '80s for who?
    Sting

Flashback Favourites

1. Who sang such classics as "Homosapien" and "Telephone Operator"?
   Pete Shelley

2. Who had a "Lost Weekend" in 1985?
   Lloyd Cole & The Commotions

3. In 1988 who had a hit with "Tears Run Rings"?
   Marc Almond

4. "Be With You" was a single from who in 1987?
   The Jack Rubies

5. Who sang the 1980 UK hit "Banana Republic"?
   Boomtown Rats

6. "The Great Commandment" was a single by who?
   Camouflage

7. This band asked "What For?" in 1988.
   James

8. "Twist" and "Go" were tracks by which Bauhaus spin-off?
   Tones On Tail

9. Whose 1988 single "Victoria" was a UK hit?
   The Fall

10. They sang "Certain Things Are Likely" in 1987.
    Kissing The Pink (KTP)

Vinyl Solutions

1. Whose debut was the UK Top 5 *White Feathers*?
Kajagoogoo

2. They followed up *Love* with *Electric.*
The Cult

3. Who released their first album *A Letter From St. Paul* in 1987?
The Silencers

4. Whose debut album was entitled *Liquidizer*?
Jesus Jones

5. *Blue* was the 1986 debut for who?
Double

6. Which American Rock band followed up their self-titled debut with the 1986 album *Shelter*?
Lone Justice

7. In 1983 who released a Synth-Pop album *With Sympathy*?
Ministry

8. *What's That Noise?* was the only hit album for who?
Coldcut

9. Which Canadian outfit released *The Rhythm Of Youth* in 1983?
Men Without Hats

10. *Silvertone* was whose 1985 debut?
Chris Isaak

Celluloid & The Box

1. The film *Less Than Zero* featured their cover of "Hazy Shade Of Winter".
   The Bangles

2. "Because Of You" was the theme from the UK TV show "Brushstrokes"- who sang it?
   Dexy's Midnight Runners

3. Whose "Love Kills" was taken from the *Sid & Nancy* sound-track?
   Joe Strummer

4. Their single "Iko Iko" was a US hit from *Rain Man.*
   Belle Stars

5. "Eye Of The Tiger" was whose massive hit from Stallone's *Rocky III*?
   Survivor

6. Who appeared in Olivia Newton-John's *Xanadu* and later had a US Top 10 with "She's A Beauty"?
   The Tubes

7. They sang "Dancing In Heaven (Orbital Be Bop)" from the Sarah Jessica Parker film *Girls Just Wanna Have Fun.*
   Q-Feel

8. Whose 1988 UK hit single "I'm Gonna Be (500 Miles)" became a massive US hit from the 1993 film *Benny And Joon*?
   The Proclaimers

9. Who did the soundtrack to the film adaptation of Orwell's *1984*?
   Eurythmics

10. Their first UK hit was the "Theme From Harry's Game" in 1982.
    Clannad

Single-Minded

1. Who sang “Rock This Town” in 1982?
   The Stray Cats

2. They had a UK hit in 1987 with “Ideal World”.
   The Christians

3. “Cry Boy Cry” was their UK Top 20 in 1982.
   Blue Zoo

4. Who first had success with “Pop Musik” in 1979?
   M

5. Their debut was the UK Top 10 “Crash”.
   The Primitives

6. The first hit “We Close Our Eyes” was their biggest.
   Go West

7. In 1987 “The Motive (Living Without You)” was their UK hit.
   Then Jerico

8. Who followed up “Good Tradition” with “Twist In My Sobriety”?
   Tanita Tikaram

9. He released consecutive UK Top 40 hits “Imagination” and “Some People” in 1986.
   Belouis Some

10. Who had a hit with “Yeh Yeh” in 1985?
    Matt Bianco

Bandstand

1. Ian Brown and John Squire were members of which successful Manchester band in the '80s?
   The Stone Roses

2. Garbage's Shirley Manson used to sing in this Edinburgh-based band.
   Goodbye Mr. Mackenzie

3. Aimee Mann used to be in which Boston band?
   Til Tuesday

4. Producer Mitch Easter founded which North Carolina band in 1981?
   Let's Active

5. UK TV presenter Richard Jobson and Stuart Adamson were members of which New Wave band?
   The Skids

6. Paul Westerberg used to front this Minneapolis band.
   The Replacements

7. Vocalist Mike Scott used to front which Celtic Rock band?
   The Waterboys

8. Juliana Hatfield used to be in which late '80s band?
   Blake Babies

9. Mark Eitzel founded which influential San Francisco band?
   American Music Club

10. Stan Ridgeway had a UK Top 5 with "Camouflage" - what was his '80s band called?
    Wall Of Voodoo

Vinyl Solutions

1. Whose only hit album in the UK was *North Of A Miracle*?
   Nick Heyward

2. *Solitude Standing* was this New Yorker's 1987 release.
   Suzanne Vega

3. Which Scottish band debuted with *Psychocandy* in 1985?
   Jesus & Mary Chain

4. They released *Battle Hymns For Children Singing* in 1983.
   Haysi Fantayzee

5. Who released *Dream Of The Blue Turtles* in 1985?
   Sting

6. Both *The Raven* and *Feline* were UK # 4 hits for who?
   The Stranglers

7. *If You Want To Defeat Your Enemy Sing His Song* was the UK Top 30 album from them.
   Icicle Works

8. This Boston band released *Hunkpapa* in 1989.
   Throwing Muses

9. *Still* and *Closer* were hit albums from which Manchester band?
   Joy Division

10. In 1989 who were *Taking On The World* with their debut?
    Gun

Flashback Favourites

1. Like the Art of Noise and Tom Jones, this noisy Leeds band covered Prince's "Kiss".
   Age Of Chance

2. Which Minneapolis band sang "Love Is The Law" in 1983?
   The Suburbs

3. This New York duo sang "Don't Let's Start".
   They Might Be Giants

4. This Scottish band sang "I Love The Things You Do To Me" in 1987.
   Balaam & The Angel

5. Whose "Collapsing New People" was a UK Indie chart Top 5 hit?
   Fad Gadget

6. "Punk Rock Girl" was a quirky number from which Philadelphia band?
   Dead Milkmen

7. Two of this band's classics were "Kiss Off" and "Blister In the Sun".
   Violent Femmes

8. Who had "Love And Pride" in '85?
   King

9. "Take The Skinheads Bowling" was a 1986 single by who?
   Camper Van Beethoven

10. This Australian outfit sang "If You Leave Me, Can I Come Too?" in 1982.
    Mental As Anything

UK # 1 Singles

1. Who sang “Geno” in 1980?
   Dexy’s Midnight Runners

2. Which Scot topped the UK charts with “Japanese Boy”?
   Aneka

3. “Never Gonna Give You Up” was his only UK chart-topper.
   Rick Astley

4. Whose Double A-side featured “Computer Love” b/w “The Model” and topped the UK chart in 1981?
   Kraftwerk

5. Their single was “Perfect” in 1988.
   Fairground Attraction

6. Who sang “Don’t Turn Around” in 1988?
   Aswad

7. “Going Underground” was the first of four # 1 hits for the Jam - name one of the other three.
   “Start”, “Town Called Malice” or “Beat Surrender”

8. In 1984 who had a # 1 with “99 Red Balloons”?
   Nena

9. Who topped the UK charts with “Brass In Pocket”?
   The Pretenders

10. “True” was a hit for who?
    Spandau Ballet

Single-Minded

1. "Love Train" and "Americanos" were both UK # 4 hits for who?
   Holly Johnson

2. Who debuted with "Shattered Dreams"?
   Johnny Hates Jazz

3. "Only The Lonely" was a US Top 10 hit for this Los Angeles band.
   The Motels

4. His debut was a hit single called "New Song".
   Howard Jones

5. Whose biggest UK hit in the '80s was "Drop The Pilot"?
   Joan Armatrading

6. Which British trio scored a debut hit with "Breakout"?
   Swing Out Sister

7. Their first hit was their biggest, "Party Fears Two" in '82.
   Associates

8. "Can Can" and "Special Brew" were both UK # 3 hits for who?
   Bad Manners

9. In 1985 who was "Running Up That Hill"?
   Kate Bush

10. Which English band had a hit with "Der Kommisar" in 1983?
    After The Fire

Vinyl Solutions

1. *Scared To Dance* and *The Absolute Game* were both UK Top 20 hits for who?
   The Skids

2. Whose debut album was *Private Revolution*?
   World Party

3. The 1988 album *The Frenz Experiment* was whose UK Top 20?
   The Fall

4. They released such UK hit albums as *Happy Families* and *Mange Tout*.
   Blancmange

5. Who were *Seduced & Abandoned* in 1987?
   Hue & Cry

6. *Ricochet Days* and *After The Snow* were albums from which English outfit?
   Modern English

7. This former Policeman called his 1987 album *X,Y,Z*.
   Andy Summers

8. Which Scottish band had *Fisherman's Blues* in 1988?
   The Waterboys

9. *People* reached # 2 in the UK for who?
   The Hothouse Flowers

10. Their 1988 album was *All That Jazz*.
    Breathe

Potluck

1. Who co-wrote "Love Like A Rocket" with Bob Geldof?
   Dave Stewart

2. He got his start selling Levi jeans and recorded the UK Top 5 hit "Each Time You Break My Heart".
   Nick Kamen

3. Who sang the Top 10 hit "Walk The Dinosaur"?
   Was (Not Was)

4. Name the Sinead O'Connor single that is featured in the film *Married To The Mob.*
   "Jump In The River"

5. There are two different singles called "Dear God", Midge Ure's one - name the other.
   XTC

6. Which beverage was Mike craving in Suicidal Tendencies' "Institutionalized"?
   A Pepsi

7. "Last Christmas" is the seasonal hit from who?
   Wham!

8. What was the name of the hit single by the Artists United Against Apartheid?
   "Sun City"

9. This 1983 Eurovision contestant went on to release the 1988 UK hit "Im Nin'Alu".
   Ofra Haza

10. Who had an album and single called *Forever Young*?
    Alphaville

Wonders Of The World

1. "The Captain Of Her Heart" was which Swiss band's hit?
   Double

2. "Doot Doot" was a moderate UK hit for who in 1983?
   Freur

3. Who had an '80s hit with the 1920's song "Puttin' On The Ritz"?
   Taco

4. "I Know There's Something Going On" was a hit for who in 1982?
   Frida

5. They nearly topped the US charts with "Keep Your Hands To Yourself".
   Georgia Satellites

6. Who had a hit "One Night In Bangkok"?
   Murray Head

7. Their only US hit was "Turning Japanese" in 1980.
   The Vapors

8. Who had a UK hit with "Magic Smile" in 1987?
   Rosie Vela

9. "10-9-8" was the only US hit for this Boston band.
   Face To Face

10. "I Can't Wait" was the only UK Top 40 hit for who?
    Nu Shooz

Single-Minded

1. They first had success with “There She Goes” in 1989.
The La’s

2. Who sang “What I Am” ?
Edie Brickell & The New Bohemians

3. “What’s On Your Mind (Pure Energy)” was the US Top 5 hit for who?
Information Society

4. Whose US hits in the ‘80s were “Don’t Dream It’s Over” and “Something So Strong”?
Crowded House

5. They had two US hits “Life In A Northern Town” and “The Love Parade”.
Dream Academy

6. “Under The Milkyway” was whose only US hit?
The Church

7. Their US hit in the ‘80s was “Tenderness”.
General Public

8. Who sang “I Love You” in 1983?
Yello

9. “I Want To Be Free” and “Thunder In The Mountains” were UK Top 10 hits for who?
Toyah

10. In 1985 who sang “Love Is Just The Great Pretender”?
Animal Nightlife

Vinyl Solutions

1. *Strip Mine* was the follow-up to their 1986 album *Stutter.*
   James

2. Whose US debut hit was *Picture This*?
   Huey Lewis & The News

3. Who was *Talking With The Taxman About Poetry* in 1986?
   Billy Bragg

4. *Reckoning* and *Fables Of The Reconstruction* were early releases from which band?
   REM

5. *Human Racing* was the first of two albums released by Nik Kershaw in 1984 - what was the second?
   The Riddle

6. *Rip It Up* was the second 1982 UK Top 40 album for who?
   Orange Juice

7. *Happy Head* and *The World Without End* are two albums from who?
   Mighty Lemon Drops

8. This Glasgow trio released *Strange Kind Of Love* in 1988.
   Love & Money

9. Whose *Kite* was a UK Top 40 hit?
   Kirsty MacColl

10. They followed up *Power, Corruption & Lies* with *Low-Life.*
    New Order

All In A Name

1. This band's name means "fast fashion" in French.
   Depêche Mode

2. What is Boy George's real name?
   George O'Dowd

3. How are Paul Hewson and Dave Evans better known?
   Bono & The Edge

4. David Robert Jones is best known as who?
   David Bowie

5. Which Liverpool band took their name from a Wild West "Wanted" poster?
   Dead Or Alive

6. Helen Folasade Adu goes by what name?
   Sade

7. This Minnesota band took their name from a Swedish board game and translates as "do you remember?".
   Hüsker Dü

8. Who is Stuart Goddard better known as?
   Adam Ant

9. Who is Georgios Kyriacos Panayiotou?
   George Michael

10. This Liverpool Synth band's name was inspired by a title of a famous Richard Bach book.
    A Flock Of Seagulls

Bandstand

1. Sisters Rose and Rachel Carlotti made up half of which Reading band?
   The Heart Throbs

2. Name the Scottish band that featured Robert Hodgens and brothers Ken and Dave McCluskey.
   The Bluebells

3. Johnny Thunders, David Johansen, Arthur Harold Kane and Sylvain Sylvain are best known as who?
   The New York Dolls

4. Malcolm McLaren created this band which featured his protégée Annabella Lu Win on vocals.
   Bow Wow Wow

5. Steve Severin and Robert Smith united for this 1983 project.
   The Glove

6. Andy McCluskey and Paul Humphreys were the core members of which British band?
   Orchestral Manoeuvres In The Dark (OMD)

7. American sisters, Tracey Bryn and Melissa Belland teamed up with Woody and Bedders from Madness to form which band?
   Voice Of The Beehive

8. Siblings Jim and William Reid are the core members of this Scottish band.
   Jesus & Mary Chain

9. In which band would you find Kate Pierson and Fred Schneider?
   The B-52's

10. What band featured Dave Stewart and Annie Lennox prior to the Eurythmics?
    The Tourists

Single-Minded

1. Whose first US hit was “Cruel Summer”?
Bananarama

2. “Anchorage” was her song from 1988.
Michelle Shocked

3. Whose first hit “Fade To Grey” was their biggest?
Visage

4. In 1988 this trio nearly had a US Top 10 with “The Promise”.
When In Rome

5. “Hey Matthew” was a UK Top 10 for who in 1987?
Karel Fialka

6. Their “We Care A Lot” single was a UK hit in 1988.
Faith No More

7. Who had a hit with “Won’t Talk About It” in 1989?
Norman Cook

8. Who was “Waiting For A Train” in 1983?
Flash & The Pan

9. Who sang “Can’t Be Sure” in 1989?
The Sundays

10. “Blue Kiss” was a single by who in 1985?
Jane Wiedlin

Vinyl Solutions

1. In 1985 *Love Not Money* was a UK Top 10 hit for who?
Everything But The Girl

2. Who followed up their self-titled debut with *Nothing's Shocking*?
Jane's Addiction

3. *Aliens Ate My Buick* was the follow-up to whose UK Top 20 *The Flat Earth*?
Thomas Dolby

4. In 1989 she followed up her self-titled debut with *Porcelain*.
Julia Fordham

5. Who followed up *Hang Ten* with *This Is Our Art* in 1988?
Soup Dragons

6. Whose 1986 debut album *Inside* featured some members of the Banshees, Heartbreakers, Bangles and Aimee Mann too?
Matthew Sweet

7. They followed up their self-titled debut with *Waiting* in 1983.
Fun Boy 3

8. At Christmas in 1985, who charted with *So The Red Rose*?
Arcadia

9. Which English Pop band followed up *Labour Of Love* with *Geffrey Morgan*?
UB40

10. Which Minnesota band released their *Let It Be* album in 1984?
The Replacements

UK # 1 Singles

1. Their only # 1 hit in the '80s was a cover of the Beatle's "With A Little Help From My Friends".
   Wet Wet Wet

2. In 1979 "I Don't Like Mondays" was a chart-topping hit for them.
   Boomtown Rats

3. "Happy Talk" jumped to the top of the charts in 1982 for who?
   Captain Sensible

4. They scored big with their cover of the Yaz(oo) hit "Only You".
   Flying Pickets

5. Who were "Too Shy" in 1983?
   Kajagoogoo

6. "If I Was" was whose # 1?
   Midge Ure

7. Their only chart-topper was a cover of Lennon's "Jealous Guy".
   Roxy Music

8. Whose debut "Ride On Time" was a UK # 1?
   Black Box

9. "The Only Way Is Up" was their # 1 in the Summer of '88.
   Yazz

10. Dead Or Alive topped the UK charts once - name it.
    "You Spin Me Round (Like A Record)"

Celluloid & The Box

1. He recorded the title track to the John Hughes film *She's Having A Baby*.
   Dave Wakeling

2. Who sang the title track to the Molly Ringwald film *Pretty In Pink*?
   Psychedelic Furs

3. From *Pretty In Pink*, whose hit "Left Of Center" featured Joe Jackson on piano?
   Suzanne Vega

4. "If You Leave" was whose hit from *Pretty In Pink?*
   Orchestral Manoeuvres In The Dark (OMD)

5. Simple Mind's "Don't You (Forget About Me)" was a hit from which Brat Pack film?
   The Breakfast Club

6. *Uncle Buck* featured whose 1988 version of "Wild Thing"?
   Tone Loc

7. Whose single "I Go Crazy" was in the film *Some Kind Of Wonderful*?
   Flesh For Lulu

8. *Say Anything* prominently featured whose track "In Your Eyes"?
   Peter Gabriel

9 Whose singles "Whistle Down The Wind" and "When It Started To Begin" are played at the dance in *16 Candles*?
   Nick Heyward

10. Name the Californian band who did the theme tune to the film *Weird Science*.
   Oingo Boingo

Potluck

1. Which guitar legend can be found on the Art of Noise's "Peter Gunn"?
   Duane Eddy

2. *Birth, School, Work, Death* is both an album and single from which Gothic band?
   The Godfathers

3. Feargal Sharkey had huge success with "A Good Heart" - who wrote it?
   Maria McKee

4. *Boys Don't Cry* is the name of both an album and single from which British band?
   The Cure

5. Whose *Fur* album spawned the hit single "Rush Hour"?
   Jane Wiedlin

6. *Happy Birthday* was both an album and single by who?
   Altered Images

7. Whose vocals are featured on Electronic's "Getting Away With It"?
   Neil Tennant (of the Pet Shop Boys)

8. Who collaborated with Clannad on "In A Lifetime"?
   Bono

9. Which popular icon directed Curiousity Killed The Cat's "Misfit" video?
   Andy Warhol

10. Who sang the UK hit "Cross That Bridge"in 1987?
    Ward Brothers

Vinyl Solutions

1. Name the Scottish band whose debut was *High Land Hard Rain.*
   Aztec Camera

2. In 1988 who had the UK Top 10 album *Close*?
   Kim Wilde

3. Whose 1981 *Anthem* was a near UK chart-topper?
   Toyah

4. *Strength* and *Declaration* were early albums by who?
   The Alarm

5. Who was *In Heat* in 1983?
   The Romantics

6. Which Glasgow band released *Raintown* in 1988?
   Deacon Blue

7. *This Is The Day, This Is The Hour, This Is This* was the 1989 release from which English band?
   Pop Will Eat Itself

8. *Whose Side Are You On?* was the debut album from who?
   Matt Bianco

9. *Candleland* was whose UK Top 20 album and featured a single of the same name?
   Ian McCulloch

10. In 1981 *Quit Dreaming And Get On The Beam* was a UK Top 10 for who?
    Bill Nelson

Answers to Quiz #38

Single-Minded

1. Which Australian outfit scored a UK Top 20 with "Hey Little Girl" in 1983?
   Icehouse

2. "Love Resurrection" and "All Cried Out" were hits for who?
   Alison Moyet

3. Who had a UK Top 5 hit with "Eloise" in 1986?
   The Damned

4. "Show Me" and "Don't Get Me Wrong" were hit singles by who?
   The Pretenders

5. "My Perfect Cousin" and "Jimmy Jimmy" were two of their UK hits.
   The Undertones

6. Whose biggest single was "The Honeythief" in 1986?
   Hipsway

7. "WFL" (aka "Wrote For Luck") was their UK chart debut in 1989.
   Happy Mondays

8. Who sang "All Around The World" in 1989?
   Lisa Stansfield

9. In 1983 they "Just Got Lucky" with a UK Top 10.
   Jo Boxers

10. Who had a hit with "Buffalo Gals" in 1982?
    Malcolm McLaren

Wonders Of The World

1. Who was at the "Breaking Point" in 1984?
   Bourgie Bourgie

2. "Dance Hall Days" was their only UK hit.
   Wang Chung

3. Who had a hit with "Rumors" in 1986?
   Timex Social Club

4. Their UK hit was "Brilliant Mind".
   Furniture

5. Who sang the US hit "I Wanna Be A Cowboy" in 1986.
   Boys Don't Cry

6. "Lets Go All The Way" was the only hit for who?
   Sly Fox

7. This Welsh band had a US Top 10 with "Cry" in 1989.
   Waterfront

8. Whose only US hit was "Perfect Way"?
   Scritti Politti

9. "Major Tom (Coming Home)" was the name of his only US hit.
   Peter Schilling

10. Who sang the quirky "Homecoming Queen's Got A Gun"?
    Julie Brown

Flashback Favourites

1. In 1982 which band released "Animal Song"?
Europeans

2. They sang a number about Brian Jones called "Godstar".
Psychic TV

3. "I Want You" was a 1985 club hit from which Sheffield band?
Cabaret Voltaire

4. Who released the single "Harley Davidson (Son Of A Bitch)" in 1986?
Bollock Brothers

5. Who sang "My Boyfriend" in 1983?
The Cucumbers

6. Whose club hit was entitled "The Dominatrix Sleeps Tonight"?
Dominatrix

7. "Einstein A Go-Go" was their 1981 UK Top 5 hit.
Landscape

8. Their first UK hit was "Down To Earth".
Curiousity Killed The Cat

9. Which Sydney quartet released "Slave Girl" in 1985?
Lime Spiders

10. They sang the 1984 single "Burning Flame".
Vitamin Z

Vinyl Solutions

1. *Please* was the UK debut hit album by who?
   Pet Shop Boys

2. *Architecture & Morality* and *Dazzle Ships* were UK Top 5 hits for who?
   Orchestral Manoeuvres In The Dark (OMD)

3. Whose debut *Diamond Life* nearly topped the UK charts?
   Sade

4. Who followed up *Rebel Yell* with *Whiplash Smile*?
   Billy Idol

5. *Doolittle* was this Boston band's 1989 album.
   Pixies

6. Who debuted with *Steps In Time*?
   King

7. They followed up *First (The Sound Of Music)* with *The Big Area* in 1989.
   Then Jerico

8. Whose debut *Spring Session M* was an anagram of their name?
   Missing Persons

9. In 1984 who had their highest charting album *It'll End In Tears*?
   This Mortal Coil

10. *Tinderbox* was the name of their 1986 album.
    Siouxie & The Banshees

UK # 1 Albums

1. Who blasted to the top of the UK charts with *Blast*?
   Holly Johnson

2. *Turn Back The Clock* was a UK # 1 from who?
   Johnny Hates Jazz

3. Who took *Into The Gap* to the top of the charts?
   The Thompson Twins

4. *Alf* was the UK chart-topper for who in 1984?
   Alison Moyet

5. Who had chart-topping *Faith* in 1987?
   George Michael

6. *Replicas*, *The Pleasure Principle* and *Telekon* were all UK # 1 albums by who?
   Gary Numan

7. *Human's Lib* was whose album which entered the UK chart in the top spot?
   Howard Jones

8. *Viva Hate* was whose solo debut and UK # 1 album?
   Morrissey

9. *Ghost In The Machine* and *Zenyatta Mondatta* were two of five consecutive UK # 1 albums by who?
   The Police

10. *Flesh & Blood* and *Avalon* were their consecutive UK chart-toppers.
    Roxy Music

Single-Minded

1. Whose single was "Too Good To Be Forgotten" in 1986?
Amazulu

2. In 1980 "Train In Vain" was the first of two US hits for who?
The Clash

3. Their single "(Feels Like) Heaven" was a UK Top 10 in 1984.
Fiction Factory

4. "Don't Forget Me (When I'm Gone)" was a hit for who in 1986?
Glass Tiger

5. "I.O.U." was nearly a UK # 1 for who in 1983?
Freeez

6. "Johnny Come Home" was their first UK hit single.
Fine Young Cannibals

7. "The Message" and "White Lines (Don't Do It)" were early '80s hits by who?
Grandmaster Flash

8. Who sang "Like The Weather" in 1987?
10,000 Maniacs

9. "Is She Really Going Out With Him?" was whose 1979 hit?
Joe Jackson

10. He had the instrumental hit "Rockit" in 1983.
Herbie Hancock

All In A Name

1. Johann Holzel was best known as what?
Falco

2. Who took their name from the "meaning of life" question in *The Hitchhiker's Guide To The Galaxy*?
Level 42

3. Which English band took their name from a 1950 award-winning film starring Bette Davis.
All About Eve

4. Patrick Murray got his start with the (English) Beat on *Special Beat Service* - how is he best known?
Pato Banton

5. This Body Snatchers off-shoot borrowed their name from a notorious female outlaw.
Belle Stars

6. How is Dublin man Fionan Hanvey best known?
Gavin Friday

7. This Human League spin-off named themselves after a group in *A Clockwork Orange*.
Heaven 17

8. This trio took their name from Hergé's famous *Tin Tin* cartoon.
The Thompson Twins

9. Her real name is Myant Myant Aye but what is her stage name?
Annabella (Lu Win)

10. What is Buster Poindexter's real name?
David Johansen

Vinyl Solutions

1. Their debut was *Lovely* and was a UK # 6 hit.
   The Primitives

2. In 1986 *Flaunt It* was whose UK Top 10?
   Sigue Sigue Sputnik

3. Whose *Blah Blah Blah* came out in 1986?
   Iggy Pop

4. Their 1985 album *Night Time* was their highest charting UK hit.
   Killing Joke

5. *Saturday Night Sunday Morning* was which Glasgow duo's 1989 album?
   River Detectives

6. *Sacred Heart* was a UK Top 10 in 1989 by who?
   Shakespear's Sister

7. Who was *Cookin' On The Roof* in 1983?
   Roman Holliday

8. *Floodland* was the 1987 UK hit from who?
   Sisters Of Mercy

9. Their album was *Too Much Pressure* in 1980.
   Selector

10. Who simply called their 1986 release *Album* and *Cassette*?
    Public Image Limited (PIL)

Bandstand

1. Who used to front Haircut 100?
   Nick Heyward

2. Political man Peter Garrett was from which Australian Rock band?
   Midnight Oil

3. David Byrne used to front this band.
   The Talking Heads

4. Bernard Sumner and Johhny Marr united under what name?
   Electronic

5. Name Siouxie and Budgie's spin-off from the Banshees.
   The Creatures

6. M People's Heather used to front this late '80s band.
   Hothouse

7. Andy Partridge is from which English band?
   XTC

8. Who founded The Teardrop Explodes before venturing off on his own in 1984?
   Julian Cope

9. Guy Chadwick fronted this English band.
   House Of Love

10. Name The The's front man.
    Matt Johnson

Celluloid & The Box

1. From *Electric Dreams*, "Together In Electric Dreams" was a near chart-topper for who?
Phillip Oakey & Giorgio Moroder

2. "Eyes Of A Stranger" was featured on the *Valley Girl* soundtrack - who sang it?
Payolas

3. *American Gigolo* featured which # 1 Blondie track?
"Call Me"

4. Who sang the US chart-topping single "St. Elmo's Fire (Man In Motion)"?
John Parr

5. The Matthew Modine film *Vision Quest* featured which massive Madonna hit?
"Crazy For You"

6. "I Do What I Do...(Theme For 9 & 1/2 Weeks)" was a US Top 40 by who?
John Taylor

7. Name the Scottish Pop-star who was in the film *Gregory's Girl*.
Clare Grogan

8. The festive film *Scrooged* featured whose "Put A Little Love In Your Heart"?
Annie Lennox (with Al Green)

9. The film *Something Wild* featured his "Man With A Gun" single.
Jerry Harrison

10. Which Ohio band sang the theme to the TV show *Square Pegs*?
The Waitresses

Flashback Favourites

1. Which Pop-Goth band sang the 1985 single “Happy Boy”?
   The Bolshoi

2. Who sang the hit single “Rapper’s Delight”?
   Sugarhill Gang

3. The single “Spiritwalker” was a UK Indie chart-topper for who?
   The Cult

4. Who was “Living On Video” in 1985?
   Trans-X

5. “Everyday (Is Halloween)” was the seasonal track by who?
   Ministry

6. Which band asked “Why Me?” in 1983?
   Planet P

7. This San Francisco Punk band sang “Holiday In Cambodia”.
   Dead Kennedy’s

8. “Let It Whip” was a US hit for who?
   Dazz Band

9. Who sang “Make A Circuit With Me”?
   The Polecats

10. “Say It Again” was a club hit by which English outfit?
    Danse Society

Vinyl Solutions

1. Whose debut album was *Let Love Rule* in 1989?
   Lenny Kravitz

2. In 1986 they had a UK hit record with *No. 10 Upping Street.*
   Big Audio Dynamite

3. The album *Bedrock Vice* was a 1987 release from who?
   Thrashing Doves

4. *Upstairs At Eric's* and *You And Me Both* were UK hits by who?
   Yaz(oo)

5. Which band's only success was with *New Clear Days* in 1980?
   The Vapors

6. Who topped the UK chart with *It's Better To Travel* in 1987?
   Swing Out Sister

7. *Wild Child* was the first full-length release from which American Ska band?
   The Untouchables

8. *Sulk* was their 1987 album and biggest UK hit.
   The Associates

9. The follow-up to *Wonderful Life* was whose 1988 album *Comedy*?
   Black

10. Who released *Radical Departure* after the split of General Public?
    Rankin' Roger

Single-Minded

1. Whose biggest UK hit was a cover of "Dear Prudence"?
Siouxie & The Banshees

2. This Ohio band sang the 1980 hit "Whip It".
Devo

3. Whose first hit "Sonic Boom Boy" was their biggest?
Westworld

4. Which quartet sang the 1981 hit single "Once In A Lifetime"?
Talking Heads

5. "Kiss This Thing Goodbye" was their only UK hit in the '80s.
Del Amitri

6. Who drove "Fast Car" up the charts?
Tracy Chapman

7. "Painted Moon" was their 1988 single.
The Silencers

8. Who sang "Goody Two Shoes"?
Adam Ant

9. They released "Me Myself And I" in 1989.
De La Soul

10. Who had early '80s hits with "Poison Arrow" and "The Look Of Love"?
ABC

Bandstand

1. Which '80s band would you associate with Kevin Rowland?
Dexy's Midnight Runners

2. After being in a Dexy's off-shoot, Mick Talbot went on to be half of which British Pop duo?
The Style Council

3. Prior to Cracker, David Lowery fronted this Northern California band.
Camper Van Beethoven

4. Mark Shaw used to front which London band?
Then Jerico

5. Bobby Gillespie left Jesus & Mary Chain to start up which band?
Primal Scream

6. Colin Newman was the founding member of which band?
Wire

7. Name the Polish singer who sang with Matt Bianco.
Basia

8. Natalie Merchant was in this Jamestown band in the '80s.
10,000 Maniacs

9. This '90s star got her break by singing on the 1989 Tears For Fears album *Seeds Of Love.*
Oleta Adams

10. Dan Baird was the lead vocalist of which Southern band?
Georgia Satellites

Celluloid & The Box

1. Whose hit "Kiss And Tell" was featured in the Michael J. Fox film *Bright Lights Big City*?
Bryan Ferry

2. The "Miami Vice" soundtrack featured their latin-titled "In Dulce Decorum" single.
The Damned

3. Their cover of the Doors' "People Are Strange" was taken from the film *The Lost Boys.*
Echo & The Bunnymen

4. Which former Squeeze member was a presenter on the British television show "The Tube"?
Jools Holland

5. He did the music for *Purple Rain* and topped the UK charts with his score for *Batman* in 1989.
Prince

6. Whose single "Gone Ridin" was in the film *American Flyers*?
Chris Isaak

7. Which British actor released the 1987 single "Generation Of Loneliness"?
Rupert Everett

8. Who recorded "Don't Box Me In" for the *Rumble Fish* soundtrack?
Stan Ridgeway & Stewart Copeland

9. In 1986 who released the title track to the Tom Hanks/Jackie Gleeson film *Nothing In Common*?
The Thompson Twins

10. The Yahoo Serious film *Young Einstein* featured their single "Great Southern Land".
Icehouse

Potluck

1. Name two bands that Vince Clarke has been a member of.
   Depêche Mode, Yaz(oo), Erasure, and The Assembly

2. Who co-wrote "China Girl"?
   David Bowie & Iggy Pop

3. They sang "Like Princes Do" in 1989.
   Diesel Park West

4. Name Rob Fisher's band prior to Climie Fisher.
   Naked Eyes

5. Who sang "Some Like It Hot" in 1985?
   The Power Station

6. It was first the title of a 1958 book, then a 1981 Jam single and finally in 1986, a film - name it.
   Absolute Beginners

7. How is John Maher best known?
   Johnny Marr

8. On what 1987 hit did Kirsty MacColl team up with the Pogues?
   "Fairytale Of New York"

9. Before Crowded House, Tim Finn and brother Neil were together in which band?
   Split Enz

10. Name two of the bands that Terry Hall has been in.
    The Specials, Fun Boy 3 and The Colour Field

Single-Minded

1. Who sang the classics "What I Like About You" and "Talking In Your Sleep"?
   The Romantics

2. "Just Like Heaven" was a US Top 40 for them in 1988.
   The Cure

3. "Don't Go" was their biggest UK hit.
   Hothouse Flowers

4. Who had "Bette Davis Eyes" in 1981?
   Kim Carnes

5. They had a UK hit with "The Harder I Try" in 1988.
   Brother Beyond

6. Who followed up their "Lifeline" with "Communication" in 1983?
   Spandau Ballet

7. "Happy Ever After" was the optimistic debut from who?
   Julia Fordham

8. Who had a huge hit with a cover of "Spirit In The Sky"?
   Doctor & The Medics

9. "Respectable" was their chart-topping single in the UK.
   Mel & Kim

10. Who teamed up with the Beatmasters for the 1989 UK Top 10 hit "I Can't Dance To That Music You're Playing"?
    Betty Boo

Vinyl Solutions

1. "Motortown" was a hit from which 1987 Kane Gang album?
Miracle

2. *Cupid & Pysche 85* was their aptly-titled 1985 release.
Scritti Politti

3. Whose US version was *Two Wheels Good* but in the UK was called *Steve McQueen*?
Prefab Sprout

4. "Saved By Zero" and "One Thing Leads To Another" can be found on this Fixx album.
Reach The Beach

5. Whose first UK hit album was called *Soul Mining*?
The The

6. This Rockabilly band was *Built For Speed* in 1982.
The Stray Cats

7. Who released *Virgins & Philistines* in 1985?
The Colour Field

8. *Night And Day* was the 1982 hit by who?
Joe Jackson

9. Their 1985 album was *Seventh Dream Of A Teenage Heaven.*
Love & Rockets

10. Whose debut album *The White Room* was released in 1989 but not a hit until 1991?
KLF

Answers to Quiz #56

Flashback Favourites

1. Who sang "Never Never" in 1983?
   The Assembly

2. Miles Copeland managed this Gothic band whose tracks included "Dance With Me" and "Open Your Eyes".
   Lords Of The New Church

3. Which American Punk band sang "Lady Killer" in the early '80s?
   The Vandals

4. Who was "Living On The Ceiling" in 1982?
   Blancmange

5. "Life Is Life" was a Euro-disco hit for them in 1987.
   Laibach

6. "Another Generation" and "Party At Ground Zero" are songs by which Californian Ska band?
   Fishbone

7. Who sang "World Destruction" in 1985?
   Time Zone

8. "Don't Crash The Car Tonight" was their 1989 track.
   Mary's Danish

9. Who released "Acceleration" in 1984?
   Bill Nelson

10. Which Los Angeles band was responsible for the patriotic track "4th Of July"?
    X

Wonders Of The World

1. Who was "The Rain" a hit for in 1986?
   Oran 'Juice' Jones

2. "Love Changes (Everything)" was their only US hit.
   Climie Fisher

3. Their only UK hit was "Safety Dance" in 1983.
   Men Without Hats

4. Annie Lennox had a huge hit with "No More 'I Love You's" - who had a UK hit with it in the '80s?
   The Lover Speaks

5. "Waiting For A Star To Fall" was their UK hit in 1988.
   Boy Meets Girl

6. Whose "Scatterlings Of Africa" was a UK hit in 1983?
   Johnny Clegg & Savuka (or Juluka)

7. They sang "Are You Sure?" in 1988.
   So

8. "Somebody's Watching Me" was the UK hit for who?
   Rockwell

9. Madonna was a one-time member of this band who sang "Right On Track".
   Breakfast Club

10. "Live It Up" was this Austalian band's only UK success.
    Mental As Anything

US # 1 Albums

1. Whose *Sports* and *Fore!* albums both spent a week on top of the US charts?
   Huey Lewis & The News

2. *The Raw & The Cooked* was the US # 1 for which English trio?
   Fine Young Cannibals

3. Whose *Songs From The Big Chair* topped the US charts?
   Tears For Fears

4. Her *Promise* album topped both the US and UK charts in 1985.
   Sade

5. *Make It Big* did just that for who in 1984?
   Wham!

6. Whose *Licensed To Ill* went to # 1 in 1986?
   Beastie Boys

7. *Beauty & The Beat* was their chart-topping debut in 1981.
   The Go-Go's

8. Whose debut *Business As Usual* was a chart-topper?
   Men At Work

9. *Synchronicity* was their only chart-topping album in the US.
   The Police

10. Mr. Mister's "Broken Wings" and "Kyrie" can be found on which # 1 album?
    Welcome To The Real World

Vinyl Solutions

1. *Escapade* was his debut solo album in 1983.
   Tim Finn

2. *Porcupine* and *Crocodiles* are two albums from which Liverpool band?
   Echo & The Bunnymen

3. *The Thin Red Line* was whose 1986 US hit album?
   Glass Tiger

4. *Beauty Stab* and *How To Be A Zillionaire* were UK hits from who?
   ABC

5. Who had a hit in 1988 with *Diesel & Dust*?
   Midnight Oil

6. Suzanne Vega was featured on whose 1989 album *Steady On*?
   Shawn Colvin

7. Whose 1984 album was *Points On The Curve*?
   Wang Chung

8. *The People Who Grinned Themselves To Death* was their second album.
   The Housemartins

9. Which Welsh band had a UK Top 40 hit with *Discover* in 1987?
   Gene Loves Jezebel

10. *Mars Needs Guitars!* and *Stoneage Romeos* were early releases from which Australian outfit?
    Hoodoo Gurus

All In A Name

1. This popular duo took their name from a "sale" sign in a furniture shop in Hull.
   Everything But The Girl

2. Who is Sally Daillon?
   Siouxie Sioux (of Banshee fame)

3. Who was the inspiration behind both Frankie Goes To Hollywood and Danny Wilson's names?
   Frank Sinatra

4. How is Bruce Robert Howard better known?
   Dr. Robert

5. Which all-girl Scottish band borrowed their name from a 1961 Elvis single?
   His Latest Flame

6. The 1964 film *The Dream Syndicate* was the inspiration behind which English band's name?
   The Dream Academy

7. How is John Mellors better known?
   Joe Strummer

8. Douglas Trendle is the larger than life frontman of Bad Manners - how is he best known?
   Buster Bloodvessel

9. They took their name from a character in the Jane Fonda film *Barbarella.*
   Duran Duran

10. How do James Osterburg's fans refer to him?
    Iggy Pop

Single-Minded

1. They sang "Lifeboat Party" and "Endicott".
   Kid Creole & The Coconuts

2. Who sang "I Ran (So Far Away)" and "Wishing (I Had A Photograph of You)"?
   A Flock Of Seagulls

3. Whose first hit single was the Einstein inspired "$E=mc^2$"?
   Big Audio Dynamite

4. Who followed up his debut chart-topper with another called "Cars"?
   Gary Numan

5. Who was "Walking On Sunshine" in 1985?
   Katrina & The Waves

6. His ode to working life was "5 O'Clock World".
   Julian Cope

7. Who sang the 1989 single"(What's Wrong With) Dreaming"?
   River City People

8. She nearly topped the UK charts in 1979 with "Lucky Number".
   Lene Lovich

9. In 1982 who released the US Top 40 hit "Valley Girl"?
   Frank Zappa (with Moon Unit)

10. Their "Love Like Blood" was a 1985 UK hit.
    Killing Joke

Bandstand

1. Who sang back up for Adam & The Ants and Dexy's Midnight Runners before releasing "Stop"?
   Sam Brown

2. This Undertones off-shoot featured the O'Neill brothers and American Steve Mack on vocals.
   That Petrol Emotion

3. Midge Ure and some Magazine men formed which Synth band?
   Visage

4. This Liverpool band featured the likes of Holly Johnson, Bill Drummond, Ian Broudie and Budgie.
   Big In Japan

5. In 1986 the line up for which band was Paul Heaton, Stan Cullimore, Norman Cook and Hugh Whitaker?
   The Housemartins

6. Keren, Sarah and Siobhan formed which trio in 1980?
   Bananarama

7. Which Dublin band featured Gavin Friday and Kik Evans (The Edge's brother)?
   The Virgin Prunes

8. Swiss men Dieter Meier and Boris Blank were known as what?
   Yello

9. Carol Decker fronted this '80s band.
   T'Pau

10. Which band featured Stewart Copeland, Stanley Clarke and Deborah Holland on vocals?
    Animal Logic

Vinyl Solutions

1. Who followed up their *Japanese Whispers* with *The Top* in 1984?
   The Cure

2. *Dream Into Action* and *One To One* were both UK Top 10 albums for who?
   Howard Jones

3. Their *Broadcast* album was a US hit in 1987.
   Cutting Crew

4. *F.L.M.* was a Top 5 album in the UK for which duo?
   Mel & Kim

5. Which band released *Correct Use Of Soap* in 1980?
   Magazine

6. His debut solo album was *Deep In The Heart Of Nowhere.*
   Bob Geldof

7. *Running In The Family* and *Staring At The Sun* were consecutive UK # 2 albums for who?
   Level 42

8. Whose first UK hit album was *Entertainment* in 1979?
   Gang Of Four

9. Their album *Bummed* was released at the end of 1989.
   Happy Mondays

10. Her UK Top 10 was *So Good* in 1988.
    Mica Paris

Flashback Favourites

1. Who sang "Russian Radio" at the end of the '80s?
   Red Flag

2. "The Lunatics (Have Taken Over The Asylum)" was the debut UK hit for who?
   Fun Boy 3

3. They sang "Everywhere I Go" and "Let The Day Begin".
   The Call

4. In 1983 who sang "Kiss Kiss Bang Bang"?
   Specimen

5. "Da Da Da" nearly topped the UK charts for this German band.
   Trio

6. Who was "Thinking Of You" in 1985?
   The Colour Field

7. Which Talking Heads spin-off had a hit with "Genius Of Love"?
   The Tom Tom Club

8. Who sang "Down Under"?
   Men At Work

9. "People Who Died" was a single by who in 1981?
   Jim Carroll

10. Who sang "88 Lines (About 44 Women)"?
    The Nails

Single-Minded

1. These Texans sang the single "The Future's So Bright I Gotta Wear Shades".
   Timbuk 3

2. "She Sells Sanctuary" was a 1985 single by who?
   The Cult

3. Who was "So Lonely" in 1980?
   The Police

4. Whose first of two US hits was "Kids In America" in 1982?
   Kim Wilde

5. Whose first UK Top 40 single was "The Rattler"?
   Goodbye Mr. Mackenzie

6. Who sang the 1987 hit "Luka"?
   Suzanne Vega

7. "King of Rock 'n' Roll" was their 1988 hit.
   Prefab Sprout

8. "Promised You A Miracle" was the first UK Top 20 for who?
   Simple Minds

9. In 1984 this Melbourne band had a US Top 40 hit "Send Me An Angel".
   Real Life

10. It was second time lucky for whose UK hit "Mary's Prayer"?
    Danny Wilson

Bandstand

1. Before The Bad Seeds, Nick Cave was in which festively-named band?
   The Birthday Party

2. At the front of which band would you find Edwyn Collins?
   Orange Juice

3. Ian McCulloch was the leader of this band.
   Echo & The Bunnymen

4. This Edinburgh man used to front Josef K.
   Paul Haig

5. Martin Fry fronted which Pop outfit?
   ABC

6. Chris Stamey and Peter Holsapple were in which New York band?
   The db's

7. Members of the early '80s Synth-band Freur resurfaced as what?
   Underworld

8. Steve Kilbey used to front which Australian band?
   The Church

9. Which band featured Morten Harket?
   A-Ha

10. Black Grape's Shaun Ryder was a founding member of what band in 1980?
    Happy Mondays

Vinyl Solutions

1. *Freedom Of Choice* was this Ohio band's US Top 40 hit in 1980.
   Devo

2. They followed up their self-titled debut with *Listen* in 1983.
   A Flock Of Seagulls

3. Which LA quintet followed up their *All Four One* with *Little Robbers* in 1983?
   The Motels

4. Name the former Buzzcock who released *Jerky Versions Of The Dream.*
   Howard Devoto

5. Who were *Shooting Rubberbands At The Stars* in 1989?
   Edie Brickell & The New Bohemians

6. Which band had only one UK hit *Big Bang* in 1989?
   We've Got A Fuzzbox And We're Gonna Use It

7. Who was *Dancing On The Couch* in 1987?
   Go West

8. The British release of their debut was called *Theodore & Friends* whilst in the US it was self-titled.
   The Adventures

9. Who released *Bête Noire* in 1987?
   Bryan Ferry

10. *The Twelve Commandments of Dance* almost topped the UK charts for who?
    The London Boys

Single-Minded

1. In 1982 who sang the US hit "We Got The Beat"?
   The Go-Gos

2. Who debuted with "Perfect Skin" in 1984?
   Lloyd Cole & The Commotions

3. "Pass The Dutchie" was a big hit by who?
   Musical Youth

4. Who took "Tour De France" into the UK charts two Summers in a row?
   Kraftwerk

5. "People Are People" was their only US hit in the '80s.
   Depêche Mode

6. Who sang "Digging Your Scene" in 1986?
   The Blow Monkeys

7. "Ghost Town" was a UK chart-topping hit by who?
   The Specials

8. Who was "Driving Away From Home" in the Spring of '86?
   It's Immaterial

9. "Electric Avenue" nearly topped the US charts for who?
   Eddy Grant

10. Who was "Oblivious" in 1983?
    Aztec Camera

Wonders Of The World

1. They sang "Whirly Girl" in 1983.
   Oxo

2. "The Politics Of Dancing" was a hit by who?
   Re-Flex

3. Name the Australian band that took "Holiday" to the Top 30 in the US.
   The Other Ones

4. "I Don't Mind At All" was this band's 1987 US hit.
   Bourgeois Tagg

5. Whose US hit was entitled "I Eat Cannibals"?
   Toto Coelo

6. Name the band and song whose only US hit was the very first video ever to be played on MTV.
   The Buggles - "Video Killed The Radio Star"

7. She choreographed *American Graffitti* and had a # 1 with "Micky" in 1982.
   Toni Basil

8. This Californian band's only US hit was "Welcome To The Boomtown".
   David & David

9. In 1988 this German band was "Keeping The Dream Alive".
   Freiheit

10. Their "Nellie The Elephant" was a UK Top 5 hit in 1984.
    Toy Dolls

Bandstand

1. Clark Datchler used to front which British Pop band?
   Johnny Hates Jazz

2. Scotsman Roddy Frame fronted this Scottish band.
   Aztec Camera

3. Paddy McAloon formed what band in 1982?
   Prefab Sprout

4. Chris Hamill (aka Limahl) was the frontman of which band?
   Kajagoogoo

5. Name either one of Kirk Brandon's bands.
   Spear Of Destiny or Theatre Of Hate

6. Name Tracy Thorn's band prior to Everything But The Girl.
   Marine Girls

7. Pete Wylie used to front this Liverpool band.
   (Mighty) Wah!

8. Luther Campbell formed this controversial Rap band in 1985.
   2 Live Crew

9. Wendy James was a co-founder of which English band?
   Transvision Vamp

10. Name the Wham! and Style Council back up singer who married Paul Weller in 1986.
    Dee C. Lee

Vinyl Solutions

1. *Tropical Gangsters* and *Doppleganger* were UK Top 40 albums by who?
   Kid Creole & The Coconuts

2. Whose most successful album was *Phantasmagoria*?
   The Damned

3. *Shabooh Shoobah* and *Listen Like Thieves* were albums by who?
   INXS

4. In 1984 *The Age Of Consent* was their debut hit album.
   Bronski Beat

5. Whose *Watermark* album was a UK # 5?
   Enya

6. Their debut *Shakespeare Alabama* was a UK Top 40 for who?
   Diesel Park West

7. In 1983 their *Touch* album went to # 1 in the UK.
   Eurythmics

8. The UK Top 40 album *Good Deeds And Dirty Rags* was whose 1989 debut?
   Goodbye Mr. Mackenzie

9. In 1985 who released the UK Top 10 album *Flaunt The Imperfection*?
   China Crisis

10. Who followed up his chart-topping debut with *Neither Fish Nor Flesh*?
    Terence Trent D'Arby

Celluloid & The Box

1. Which Gothic band had a cameo performance in David Bowie's *The Hunger*?
   Bauhaus

2. *True Stories* was the name of their film and album in 1986.
   Talking Heads

3. In 1988 which band released "Doctorin' The Tardis" a tribute to the cult TV show "Dr Who"?
   Timelords

4. *Do The Right Thing* featured whose "Fight The Power"?
   Public Enemy

5. In 1980 the film *Rude Boy* featured this band.
   The Clash

6. The American sitcom "Get A Life" had this band's "Stand" as the theme song.
   REM

7. This trio featured members of the Beat and took their name from a 1960 MGM film.
   Fine Young Cannibals

8. Which Welsh band took their name from a TV show in Britain and debuted with *Pop Said*?
   Darling Buds

9. A "Star Trek" Vulcan princess was the inspiration for their name.
   T'Pau

10. Who played the charactor May Day in the James Bond film *A View To A Kill*?
    Grace Jones

Single-Minded

1. Who sang "Underneath The Radar"?
   Underworld

2. Which band featured the computer-generated Max Headroom on their "Paranoimia" single?
   Art Of Noise

3. "Sunglasses At Night" was whose 1984 US Top 10?
   Corey Hart

4. "Stand By" and "Don't Try To Stop It" were 1983 singles by who?
   Roman Holliday

5. Who sang the chart-topping hit "Rock Me Amadeus" in 1986?
   Falco

6. Which English band sang "Martha's Harbour"?
   All About Eve

7. "She Bangs The Drums" was the first UK hit by who?
   The Stone Roses

8. Who had a US # 1 with "Toy Soldiers" in 1989?
   Martika

9. "Everyday Is Like Sunday" was the follow-up to whose "Suedehead"?
   Morrissey

10. Who released the 1981 UK Top 5 hits "Souvenir" and "Joan Of Arc"?
    Orchestral Manoeuvres In The Dark (OMD)

Bandstand

1. Martha Davis was the leader of this LA band.
The Motels

2. Hugh Cornwell was the lead singer in which band?
The Stranglers

3. Boo Hewerdine was in which Cambridge-based band?
The Bible

4. What is the name of Robert Smith's band?
The Cure

5. This Californian band featured Exene Cervenka and John Doe.
X

6. Sinead O'Connor was briefly a member of which band?
In Tua Nua

7. Mancrab was an off-shoot of which English outfit?
Tears For Fears

8. Johnette Napolitano fronted which Los Angeles Rock band?
Concrete Blonde

9. In the late '70s and early '80s, Pete Shelley was in which Punk band?
The Buzzcocks

10. Name the popular duo that were once back up singers for Wham.
Pepsi & Shirley

Flashback Favourites

1. He released a single called "Vertigo" in 1989.
Matthew Sweet

2. Who had a "Mirror In The Bathroom" in 1980?
The (English) Beat

3. "Never Say Never" and "A Girl In Trouble" were two singles from which San Francisco band?
Romeo Void

4. They had moderate success with "Eardrum Buzz" in the Spring of '89.
Wire

5. Which Cleveland band was "Waiting For Mary" in 1989?
Pere Ubu

6. In 1986 this band released "One Simple Thing".
The Stabilizers

7. Who sang "China" in 1983?
Red Rockers

8. "Wordy Rappinghood" was a 1981 UK hit from who?
Tom Tom Club

9. "Everywhere That I'm Not" and "No Time Like Now" are tracks by which Californian band?
Translator

10. In 1986 whose "Suzi's On The Ball Now" single was produced by Ian Broudie?
The Three O'Clock

Potluck

1. U2's The Edge teamed up with who to release "Heroine (Theme From Captive)"?
   Sinead O'Connor

2. Prior to his stint as an MTV Europe VJ, what band was Miles Hunt in?
   The Wonderstuff

3. Which prestigious label was the early home to the likes of Edwyn Collins and Aztec Camera?
   Postcard Records

4. Name the two bands you associate with Jimmy Somerville.
   Bronski Beat & The Communards

5. Band Aid's "Do They Know It's Christmas" went straight to # 1 in the UK - who wrote it?
   Bob Geldof & Midge Ure

6. The Hothouse Flowers helped out on whose "Closer To Fine" single?
   Indigo Girls

7. There were two versions of this Peter Gabriel song - one was sung in German.
   "Shock The Monkey"

8. Which 1979 album did *Rolling Stone* critics deem the "Album Of The '80s"?
   The Clash - *London Calling*

9. *World Shut Your Mouth* was whose UK Top 40 solo album and single?
   Julian Cope

10. Members of UB40, Madness and General Public got together to record which 1985 Ethopian famine-relief single?
    "Starvation"

Vinyl Solutions

1. In 1979 who released *Valley Of The Dolls*?
Generation X

2. Which Finnish rockers had a UK Top 40 album with *Two Steps From the Move*?
Hanoi Rocks

3. Whose *The Big Lad In The Windmill* was their most successful album?
It Bites!

4. In 1988 their album *Little Children* nearly topped the UK charts.
The Mission

5. *Darklands* and *Barbed Wire Kisses* were UK Top 10 albums for who?
Jesus & Mary Chain

6. Whose *A Word To The Wise Guy* was a 1984 UK Top 30 album?
Mighty Wah!

7. *If I Should Fall From Grace With God* was a Top 5 in the UK for who?
The Pogues

8. In 1980 who had *Seconds Of Pleasure* with a UK Top 30 album?
Rockpile

9. Which outfit was *Hypnotised* with their UK Top 10 album in 1980?
The Undertones

10. Whose UK hit album was *Sold* in 1987?
Boy George

Single-Minded

1. Their first hit single was "Tell That Girl To Shut Up".
   Transvision Vamp

2. In 1985 they released "I Thought I'd Never See You Again" and "Sweet Nothing".
   Working Week

3. They released the UK hit "Respect Yourself" in 1984.
   The Kane Gang

4. "I Don't Want A Lover" was whose debut single?
   Texas

5. Their "Give A Little Love" nearly topped the UK chart.
   Aswad

6. Who released "Return To Yesterday" in 1988?
   The Lilac Time

7. Whose "Sit Down" was first released in the Summer of '89?
   James

8. "There's A Ghost In My House" was a UK Top 30 in 1987 for who?
   The Fall

9. Who sang "I Know What Boys Like" in 1982?
   The Waitresses

10. "Sweetest Smile" was whose UK Top 10?
    Black

US # 1 Singles

1. Which London-based band sang "Wild Wild West" in 1988?
The Escape Club

2. The Bangles had two chart-toppers - name either one.
"Eternal Flame" and "Walk Like An Egyptian"

3. Whose cover of the Hall & Oates' hit "Everytime You Go Away" was a chart-topper?
Paul Young

4. Formerly the leader of the Baby's, who sang "Missing You"?
John Waite

5. U2 had two US chart-topping hits in the '80s - name either one.
"I Still Haven't Found What I'm Looking For" or "With Or Without You"

6. Which Australian sang "Jessie's Girl" in 1981?
Rick Springfield

7. Who topped the US charts with a cover of "You Keep Me Hanging On"?
Kim Wilde

8. Shocking Blue topped the US charts with "Venus" in 1969 - who did the same with it in 1986?
Bananarama

9. "(I Just Died) In Your Arms" was whose # 1 hit?
Cutting Crew

10. The first two US hits by Tears For Fears topped the charts - name either one.
"Everybody Wants To Rule The World" and "Shout"

Bandstand

1. The Dukes of Stratosphear was the alter ego of which English band?
   XTC

2. Mike Edwards formed which band in 1988?
   Jesus Jones

3. Which English group features Harriet Wheeler's vocals?
   The Sundays

4. Roland Gift was the lead singer of which band?
   Fine Young Cannibals

5. In which Dublin band would you find Liam O'Maonlai?
   The Hothouse Flowers

6. Graham Skinner and Pim Jones were founding members of which Glasgow Pop band?
   Hipsway

7. Which influential band did Chuck Prophet join in 1984?
   Green On Red

8. Gary Daly and Eddie Lundon formed which band in Merseyside in 1979?
   China Crisis

9. Which trio featured Ian Marsh, Martyn Ware and Glenn Gregory on vocals?
   Heaven 17

10. Raintree Crow features some original members of which '80s band?
    Japan

Vinyl Solutions

1. *Pleasure Victim* was the US debut for who?
   Berlin

2. Who went to # 2 in the UK with *Too Rye Aye*?
   Dexy's Midnight Runners

3. *New York* was whose biggest UK hit from the '80s?
   Lou Reed

4. Whose only UK hit was *Laughing At The Pieces*?
   Doctor & The Medics

5. *Angst In My Pants* was this Californian band's 1982 album.
   Sparks

6. They followed up their self-titled debut with *Gatecrashing* in 1989.
   Living In A Box

7. Whose 1986 album was *Animal Magic*?
   The Blow Monkeys

8. In 1980 who was *Flogging A Dead Horse*?
   Sex Pistols

9. Their album *Like Gangbusters* went Top 20 in the UK in 1983.
   Jo Boxers

10. All of their albums were UK Top 10 hits, and in 1980 it was *Vienna*.
    Ultravox

Potluck

1. "Kiss Me" was the 1985 UK Top 5 from who?
Stephen "Tin Tin" Duffy

2. In Tommy Tutone's song, what was Jenny's telephone number?
867-5309

3. "She Blinded Me With Science" was whose only US hit?
Thomas Dolby

4. Who sang the 1988 UK hit single "Joe Le Taxi"?
Vanessa Paradis

5. "Wheels Of Wonder" and "Healing At The Harbour" were 1989 singles by which Glasgow Rock band?
Kevin McDermott Orchestra

6. Klark Kent was the alter ego of who?
Stewart Copeland

7. They followed up their debut US hit single "And We Danced" with 1986's "Day By Day".
The Hooters

8. Who sang the 1979 UK hit "Are Friends Electric"?
Tubeway Army (aka Gary Numan)

9. Which 1985 Smiths' hit did Soho sample for their 1990 hit "Hippy Chick"?
"How Soon Is Now?"

10. Who sang "I Melt With You"?
Modern English

Flashback Favourites

1. Who sang the UK Top 40 hit "Free Yourself"?
   The Untouchables

2. They sang "Numbers With Wings" and "Barbarella".
   The Bongos

3. "Biting My Nails" was a single by who?
   Renegade Soundwave

4. "I Touch Roses" and "Boy" were singles by which Los Angeles band?
   Book Of Love

5. This band sang "Eighties" in 1984.
   Killing Joke

6. This Fall off-shoot were "Waking Up In The Sun" in 1989.
   Adult Net

7. Who had a US hit in 1983 with "Twilight Zone"?
   Golden Earring

8. "Don't Sniff Coke" was a single by who?
   Pato Banton

9. Who released the raunchy dance club hit "Tastes So Good" in 1984?
   File 13

10. "Independence Day" was a single from which Sheffield band?
    Comsat Angels (aka CS Angels)

Singled-Minded

1. Whose first UK hit single was "Song For Whoever"?
Beautiful South

2. "Heaven (Must Be There)" and "Can't Wait To See You" are singles from which Australian band?
Eurogliders

3. "Chuck E's In Love" was a hit in both the US and UK for who?
Ricki Lee Jones

4. "When Will I Be Famous?" was their 1988 UK # 1.
Bros

5. Whose first US hit was "Do You Believe In Love"?
Huey Lewis & The News

6. "I Got You" was the 1980 UK hit by who?
Split Enz

7. Who took "One Step Beyond" into the UK charts in 1979?
Madness

8. Whose UK debut hit was entitled "Wishing I Was Lucky"?
Wet Wet Wet

9. "Yeah Yeah Yeah Yeah Yeah" was a 1988 single by who?
The Pogues

10. Whose UK debut was the Top 10 single "My One Temptation"?
Mica Paris

Bandstand

1. Colin Vearncombe was the core member of this Liverpool band.
   Black

2. Singer Mike Peters fronted this Welsh Rock band.
   The Alarm

3. Bob Mould founded which band in 1979?
   Hüsker Dü

4. Susanna Hoffs was in which band?
   The Bangles

5. Who was the Television frontman that released "A Town Called Walker" in 1987?
   Tom Verlaine

6. Dali's Car consisted of who?
   Peter Murphy and Mick Karn

7. Johnny McElhone of Texas got his start in which Scottish Pop band?
   Altered Images

8. Michael Hutchence was the lead singer of which Australian band?
   INXS

9. Name the legendary outfit that was co-founded by Joe Strummer.
   The Clash

10. Gary Clark was from which Scottish band?
    Danny Wilson

UK # 1 Albums

1. *Sparkle In The Rain* was the first of four consecutive UK chart-toppers for who?
   Simple Minds

2. *Never For Ever* was whose UK # 1?
   Kate Bush

3. *Colour By Numbers* was the only chart-topping hit for who?
   Culture Club

4. Their debut *Lexicon Of Love* was whose chart-topper?
   ABC

5. *Eat To The Beat* was whose UK # 1 album in 1979?
   Blondie

6. *When The World Knows Your Name* was this Glasgow band's chart-topping second release.
   Deacon Blue

7. In 1987 *Keep Your Distance* was a chart-topping hit for this London quartet.
   Curiousity Killed The Cat

8. Whose 1980 album was *Kings Of The Wild Frontier*?
   Adam & The Ants

9. Their only chart-topping UK album was *Steeltown* in 1984.
   Big Country

10. *The Innocents* and *Wild!* both topped the UK chart for who?
    Erasure

Single-Minded

1. Who had a big hit with their "Hands To Heaven" in 1988?
   Breathe

2. "Alone Without You" was a UK Top 10 in 1985 for who?
   King

3. They sang "Graceland" in 1989.
   The Bible

4. "Shiny Shiny" was their 1983 UK hit.
   Haysi Fantayzee

5. Who sang "Here Comes Your Man" in 1989?
   The Pixies

6. In 1983 "(Keep Feeling) Fascination" was a massive hit for them.
   Human League

7. Whose debut was the UK smash hit "Love Missile F1-11"?
   Sigue Sigue Sputnik

8. Who had the UK Top 5 "Sign Of The Times" in 1983?
   Belle Stars

9. "Walking In L.A." and "Destination Unknown" were tracks by who?
   Missing Persons

10. Who sang the classic track "Blue Monday"?
    New Order

Potluck

1. Henry Rollins left which seminal punk band in 1986 to embark on a solo career?
   Black Flag

2. Who got together to record "Change Your Mind" in 1985?
   Gary Numan with Bill Sharpe (Sharpe & Numan)

3. This Scottish band sang "The Whole Of The Moon" in 1985.
   The Waterboys

4. Who sang "I Want You Back" in 1983?
   The Hoodoo Gurus

5. The film *The Krays* starred the Kemp brothers - name their '80s band.
   Spandau Ballet

6. Who had a hit with "Our Lips Are Sealed"?
   Trick Question! US: The Go-Go's UK: Fun Boy 3

7. They collaborated on "Don't Give Up".
   Peter Gabriel and Kate Bush

8. Who is Robert Fripp's famous wife?
   Toyah

9. Dusty Springfield helped out on their single "What Have I Done To Deserve This?".
   Pet Shop Boys

10. They sang the UK Top 10 hits "Heaven Knows I'm Miserable Now" and "Sheila Take A Bow".
    The Smiths

Vinyl Solutions

1. *Wha'appen* was whose follow-up to *I Just Can't Stop It*?
   The (English) Beat

2. In 1986 their *Victorialand* was a UK Top 10.
   Cocteau Twins

3. Whose *Stuck In Wonderamaland* came out in 1989?
   Dramarama

4. They released *The Eight Legged Groove Machine* in 1988.
   The Wonderstuff

5. In 1989 who released their greatest hits album *Pastpresent*?
   Clannad

6. Who released the 1984 UK Top 40 album *Heaven Is Waiting*?
   Danse Society

7. *Raw Like Sushi* was a UK # 2 for who?
   Neneh Cherry

8. *The Ups And Downs* was whose UK Top 40 album in 1985?
   Stephen "Tin Tin" Duffy

9. *Rattlesnakes* was the 1984 debut from who?
   Lloyd Cole & The Commotions

10. Who released *Whammy!* in 1983?
    The B-52's

Under-Cover

1. They had a UK Top 5 with a funky version of "Money".
Flying Lizzards

2. This band sampled "New Years Day" on their "A Bif Of..." single.
Kiss AMC

3. Who had a UK hit with their version of "I Want Candy"?
Bow Wow Wow

4. Their cover of "Ball Of Confusion" was a dance club hit.
Love & Rockets

5. Whose "Always Something There To Remind Me" was a US Top 10 hit in 1983?
Naked Eyes

6. Who had a UK Top 5 hit with a cover of "Wild World" in 1988?
Maxi Priest

7. Name the gothic band who did a zany version of "Like A Virgin".
Lords Of The New Church

8. This band had a hit with Neil Diamond's "Red Red Wine".
UB40

9. Name the Glasgow duo who covered Kate Bush's "Man With A Child In His Eyes".
Hue & Cry

10. Who had a UK # 1 in '81 with their cover of "Tainted Love"?
Soft Cell

Great Sources of Help

Beech, Mark. *The A-Z of Names In Rock*: (1998).

Christgau, Robert. *Christgau's Record Guide: The '80s*: (1990).

Dafydd, Rees and Luke Crampton, *The Guinness Book of Rock Stars*: (1991).

Davies, Chirs. *British & American Hit Singles: 1946-1997*: (1998)

Gambaccini, Paul, Jonathon Rice, and Tim Rice. *The Guinness Book of British Hit Albums*: (1996).

Gambaccini, Paul, Jonathon Rice, and Tim Rice. *The Guinness Book of British Hit Singles*: (1995).

Larkin, Colin. *The Virgin Encyclopedia*: (1997).

Larkin, Colin. *The Guinness Who's Who of Indie & New Wave Music*: (1992).

Lazzell, Barry. *Indie Hits 1980 -1989*: (1997).

McAleer, Dave. *The Warner Guide to UK & US Hit Singles*: (1996).

Whitburn, Joel. *The Billboard Book of Top 40 Hits*: (1996).

Whitburn, Joel. *The Billboard Book of Top 40 Albums*: (1991).

Again, whilst every effort was taken to ensure that the questions and answers are accurate, they are only as good as my sources. Sometimes there were even discrepancies within the reference books, at which point it had to be a judgement call. If you have found anything that was blatantly wrong, please email the question to:

essential-80s@mailcity.com

Thea Newcomb has worked in Marketing and Promotion for both major and independent record labels in the US. She was trained to degree level in Broadcasting at Sonoma State University in her native state of California. Since settling in the UK, Thea has acquired several years of radio experience - presenting music shows at both a local and regional level in Scotland. Thea's musical career has also spanned to journalism where she was a regular contributor to M8 magazine and went on to co-found Bigwig magazine. Career highlights include interviewing a wide array of artists from Hootie & The Blowfish to A House and co-presenting shows with the likes of Jane Wiedlin and Kevin McDermott. Thea is happily living in Glasgow with her partner Derick, and is currently working on her second book.